YOUNG MUDDLED

A Memoir

bancroft
press

ROBERT KANIGEL

Cover Design: Jacqueline Tobin (www.hugejam.com)
Interior Design: tracycopescreative.com

978-1-61088-552-2 (HC)
978-1-61088-553-9 (PB)
978-1-61088-554-6 (Ebook)
978-1-61088-555-3 (PDF)
978-1-61088-556-0 (Audiobook)

Published by Bancroft Press
"Books that Enlighten"
(818) 275-3061
4527 Glenwood Avenue
La Crescenta, CA 91214
www.bancroftpress.com

Printed in the United States of America

ALSO BY ROBERT KANIGEL

Hearing Homer's Song

Eyes on the Street

On an Irish Island

Faux Real

High Season

Vintage Reading

The One Best Way

The Man Who Knew Infinity

Apprentice to Genius

For young David, Dashiell, Trevor,

Ulysses, Sonia, Ben, and Barry

1

It was 1966 and I was fresh out of school, newly landed in Baltimore. A war was going on in Vietnam, but for me life was good. You'd have thought so, too, after four years of stress analysis and heat transfer and only the barest sprinkling of Hemingway or Beckett. Now I had my first real job. I was making money. I could go down to Sherman's Book Store and buy all the books I wanted and not worry they'd distract me from studying for the next exam. I had a car, a battered old Peugeot 403, like the one Peter Falk later made memorable in the Columbo TV series. A few weeks before, I'd turned 20; I was ignorantly, happily young. Ahead of me were Life, and girls, or women, or whatever we called them then, and my fine new job.

But in the few years after I arrived in Baltimore, my life turned abruptly on itself, twisted away from the past, never returning to the familiar thing it had been: I left a job I could no longer bear. I fell in love. I became a writer. This is the story of how, along the rowhouse-lined streets of Baltimore and the great, gray boulevards of Paris, I was remade into a new life. And it's the story of my old life, too, and how, with each fitful and confused step away from it, sometimes hurting myself and others along the way, I stumbled onto a path more naturally, more truly, my own.

By now it borders on a snarky, over-told joke to say that, these days, the personal memoir has become a bastion for harrowing tales of childhood abuse, addiction, recovery, adventures in exotic places, and every kind and degree of misery, crime, or excess; or else, that it has become a second home for rock stars and celebrities. This is a cartoonish breakdown, one overlooking real distinctions between the bad, the good, and the great. Still, it's more true than not that memoirs today turn their backs on the ordinary and the familiar.

The story I tell here mostly plays out in this often unloved landscape. It embodies much youthful confusion, heartbreak, and foolishness, set against a tumultuous period in the nation's life. But the tumult lies mostly offstage. And the mistakes I made, the paths I followed, didn't leave me with needle tracks or in jail. My account is not of depravity, trauma, or threatened death—if for the moment we exclude the frequent outcome, in 1968, of being shipped off to Vietnam.

My story is not one of life and death, but of love and work.

In the wake of those exhilarating few years of the late 1960s, and across my whole adult life since, I've been a writer of articles, essays, and books. Even in the early days, I wrote articles about everything— movie censorship, longshoremen, the *Whole Earth*

Catalog, bar owners and bike racers, modern physics and old books.

Having served an apprenticeship of sorts, over the next three decades I wrote books, nine of them, which took me to Europe and Asia and across the reaches of the centuries, to research and to write. One was adapted for a film featuring international stars you may have heard of, and has been translated into more than fifteen languages. Another was the basis for a public television documentary. Several earned fellowships or awards, or splashy reviews in national magazines, or respectful appraisals in scholarly journals.

Others sank without trace. Their modest first printings were their only printings. They were read by a scant few of those interested in whatever outlandish topic I had chosen to write about, and no one else. Sometimes my books got cruel reviews. Sometimes they were just ignored.

Altogether, with the highs and the lows, the hits and misses, maybe I inhabit the broad middle rank of working nonfiction writers. I've made a living from my work and, after early struggles, have managed a middle class-enough life. Enough, anyway, to keep on keeping on.

But that's now. In 1966, I could not have imagined my life playing out as it has. That I would do the work I do. Or love the women I loved. My life and work seemed laid out for me, the future a detailed roadmap. The map was wrong.

Baltimore then was more like our time than not, though set to the dark bass notes, as the whole country was, of the Vietnam War. America was on its 36th president; we're up to 46 today. There were McDonalds, just as now; millions of cars on the roads, but not so many millions; and computers, too, though they fit in rooms, not palms. It was the time of the first moon landing, which President Kennedy had made the nation's goal a few years before; we haven't been back since, more than half a century later. But people worked, played, dreamed, loved: The time-traveler would find contrasts, but American life's broad landscape would be familiar.

And yet the very air was changing.

The Sixties are forever shackled to their vivid and disruptive events. So much happened. So much spun around, so fast. There were demonstrations and tear gas, hippies and ridiculous outfits and wild color and peculiar newspaper fonts and amazing music and marijuana and sex everywhere, and the war—always the goddamn senseless war.

As much changed internally as externally. The Sixties were about the world opening up for us, about *possibility*. They were a time when chaotic events pressed hard against everyday assumptions and aspirations. A time when the sheer pressure of new ideas challenged middle-class life as so many millions, like me, had been prepared to accept it only a few years before. The Sixties swept our confused young lives onto new paths. That's what happened to me, and that's the story this book tells.

2

It was June 1966, three days following my college graduation. After a two hundred mile drive down from Brooklyn, I turned off the expressway and headed south, into Baltimore. York Road started open and broad as it dropped down from the Beltway, but soon congealed into a clutter of roadside car repair shops and fast-food restaurants. Heat bubbled up from the street, which soon had a new name, Greenmount Avenue, and the faces turned black. It was late afternoon by now, but the sun was still high in the sky. I had the car windows open wide, but they let in only more of the hot, close, cloistered air of a Baltimore summer.

I finally had to stop, get out of the car, and find out where I was. I parked and found a lone bench squeezed onto a narrow downtown sidewalk and planted my wilted self on it. Right there, amidst all the heat and traffic, I took what felt like my first deep breath of the day and hauled out a map. A few blocks away was the Alcazar hotel, eight stories with big plate-glass windows lined up along Cathedral Street, with a famous ballroom that used to get all the big traveling bands in its Twenties heyday. Now, 40 years past its prime, it was a hotel for single gentlemen, which is what I was for the night.

I checked in, got a room key, waited for the elevator attendant to take up his station, close the cage behind us, and whisk me up to my room. He was about my age, but knowing beyond his years. What was I doing in town? he wanted to know. Bound for The Block was I? he said with a wink: Burlesque houses, with girls, girls, brassy big-breasted ones. I didn't say much. I was still a virgin. I looked down at the elevator floor.

Then I was in my little room, on my narrow bed, in the heat, my tinny portable radio playing "Eve of Destruction."

Next day, I checked the newspaper ads for apartments to rent, got some addresses, and headed off in the car. Before I'd gotten very far, still downtown, I turned onto Calvert Street and, bound north, found myself flanked by street-hugging rows of four- and five-story brownstone majesties, rhythms of walls and windows, beautiful. Well, no, not beautiful. Or maybe yes, beautiful. What, exactly, could be beautiful about a city street? Surely, though, it bore a harmony to which I responded, even if I couldn't name or understand it.

Then, a sign, hung on a red door just below Eager Street: APARTMENT FOR RENT. I was bound for somewhere else, I had an address, a place out in the suburbs to inspect. But just five minutes from the Alcazar, I pulled over, parked, approached the red door, and knocked. The door opened with a blast of air-conditioned cold, and I was ushered into the office, a stone wall's thickness off the sidewalk, of Mr. Ludwig Heidler.

Or maybe it was Dr. Ludwig Heidler; it must have been, since he was learned in all things. He was a little man in his sixties, in a dark suit and tie, with a black mustache and a balding pate he covered over, as best I could see, with shoe polish. The apartment he had to rent was in the basement of a five-story brownstone in the next block. The people were just moving out. It would be great for me, he said. At just $90 a month. *And*, he lifted an eyebrow, the top floor unit was home to a young single woman I was sure to be interested in. She was good looking. She got around; he knew this for a fact; Mr. Heidler knew everything for a fact, said everything with a leer. This little mustachioed man, I was meant to conclude, knew about women, knew about books, knew about languages, the entirety of his patter an embodiment of perfect knowledge. Even to me, just turned twenty, this wasn't wholly convincing.

I wouldn't be able to see the place just now, as the current residents would be there for a few days yet. Still, I said I'd take it. I never saw the other apartments I'd arranged to see. Never got out of downtown.

Never got off Calvert Street.

⌣‒‒‒

My new job wasn't to start for a week or two, I had some time, so a few days later I thought I'd drop by the apartment and get a peek at it. It was half a block up from Heidler's office, set a few steps down and back from the sidewalk, offering a big, brightly painted door to the world. Beside it, set into the thick stone, was a frosted window that was the place's only source of natural light. I knocked, preparing to introduce myself.

The young man who opened the door was a few years older than I, tall, thin—way too thin, it seemed to me—with acne pustules riddling his pasty white face. His name was Edwin and, as he told me early in our brief acquaintance and without hesitation, he was a male hustler. He made his living at the western edge of a nearby park, picking up men looking for sex and stealing their money. He hung out with a group of like-minded friends who lived together in an apartment a block over on St. Paul Street. Edwin soon took me to meet his friends, all in their twenties and, to my untutored eye, of inscrutable sexual bent.

Somehow, the disreputable underworld in which I found myself did not feel threatening. Not thanks to any poise or street smarts on my part. Rather, I suspect, because my new acquaintances seemed so easy with each other, saw me as too young and inexperienced to treat as anything but boy-man curiosity; besides, Edwin vouched for me. Whatever they were up to when they ranged through the city at night, they were cheerful and light when I saw them during the day. It was as if I'd been adopted, as a pet.

Whatever Edwin's sexual proclivities, the person he lived with in the dark, low-ceilinged apartment that was soon to be mine was a girl, Merrily, in her mid-teens. Maybe a runaway, I guessed, though I didn't know what a runaway was supposed to look like. Fair, slim and slight, she wore hardly a thing that Baltimore summer—the flimsiest of tops, the shortest of shorts, rarely shoes, even on the hot sidewalks. A few days after I met them, she stepped on a nail and I had to drive her down to the Mercy Hospital emergency room. There I got to know her a little, though I never learned where she was from or much about her relationship with Edwin, except that they seemed together, as a couple, sort of. I surmised she was escaping from something and that here, in downtown Baltimore, she'd found what she needed.

In Merrily's mental cosmos, Downtown—she always said it with a capital D—loomed large. Downtown you could do anything. Downtown was where you could be free. I don't know how well this went for downtown Baltimore, which was no Greenwich Village or swinging SoHo. Nor did it say much for

Merrily's originality: The year before, a British singer, Petula Clark, had come out with a catchy megahit, "Downtown": "So go downtown/things will be great when you're downtown." I ingested some of this adolescent civic boosterism, too: Downtown was where it was happening, baby. And whatever she was running away from, some gritty hick town or empty, sterile suburb, was nowhere I wanted to be either.

Anyway, in a week or so, during which time Edwin went through the ceremony of bestowing on me his business card, he and Merrily cleared out their few belongings and I moved in. I never saw either of them again. Soon, though, I was lapping up a good, trashy paperback, entitled *Uptown Downtown*: "By day," the cover advised, "he was a ruthless executive, by night a free-wheeling beatnik. He had the best of both worlds...and the perfect woman in each."

In Baltimore, I felt in the middle of things—as much as you could feel in the middle of things in Baltimore, already well into a postwar decline that would never manage to dull my affection for it. My apartment was a few blocks from Mt. Vernon Place, with its stately monument to George Washington, dating to 1829, at its center, and surrounded by the city's most enduring cultural monuments. There was the great stone edifice of the Walters Art Museum, at the time still formally termed a "gallery"; and the Peabody Conservatory, whose students you could hear from the park practicing their arpeggios in spring and summer; and a few blocks up, the hulking mass of the Sheraton Belvedere hotel, where F. Scott Fitzgerald famously went to drink.

There were eateries and bars; and, by 1966, the first hints of the coming counterculture, with its head shops and underground newspapers, in a few colorful storefronts along Read Street. On Sunday mornings, I'd walk over to the Belvedere to buy a copy of the Sunday *New York Times*. I'd had to *learn* to do that; it was not at first obvious to me, a native New Yorker, that a New York City paper might not be available on every Baltimore street corner.

One time soon after I got to town, I walked into a luncheonette on Charles Street, its long soda fountain retreating back from the street, and asked for an egg cream. The young woman behind the counter stood there, looking at me blankly. "A what?" she asked.

"An egg cream," I said

"What's that?" she asked again.

An egg cream contains no egg and no cream, but boasts a milky head, punctured by a brown dot of chocolate syrup, stirred and frothed up with seltzer—a chocolate ice cream soda without the ice cream. The young Baltimore woman behind the counter deserved an explanation something like that. But my

New York provincialism ran so deep I couldn't supply one. I literally didn't understand her question: How could you ask what an egg cream was? An egg cream was an egg cream, period, staff of life to every New Yorker of my generation, available at any corner candy store.

Alerted to an awkward scene in the making, someone else behind the counter stepped in to help. But she didn't know what I was talking about either. I tried to explain, failed, and—this deficit of Baltimore life simply beyond my comprehension—just left.

But soon, for all my bludgeon-headed obtuseness, and all of Baltimore's quaint limitations, I fell into the life of the city. For one thing, Joanne, the young woman Mr. Heidler had mentioned, really existed, in the garret apartment six flights up from mine. Soon I met her, and almost as soon, though we were never really a couple, we had coupled, I for the first time. Joanne was a social worker, dark-haired and pretty, a few years older than I, with lots of friends and wide interests.

My first act of sexual intercourse, a few weeks after I'd turned twenty, happened in my grimly dark apartment, where, when it was over, Joanne asked, "Was this your first time?" I don't remember much beyond that; who'd want to after that? But the second time, upstairs in her place high over Calvert Street, just within the window bay, I remember clearly—lying there beside her in languorous leisure afterwards, the wetness and heat of her, its sheer plenty a revelation to me.

Especially because I was no longer an adolescent— I was out of college, for goodness' sake—these early sexual fumblings might have left a self-conscious taint on my first weeks in Baltimore. But they didn't; they were OK. Pretty quickly I could see that sex was fraught, that the whole business had its stock of little indignities, that along with it being about the best thing in the world, it was the silliest damn thing, too, with its messy mixing of limbs and liquids, its blurps and grunts, and the inevitability with which one felt in its thrall. But it was just fine, really, and entirely worth it, and enormous fun, an extravagant and warming pleasure. I decided I need not be too embarrassed by my early inexperience, ignorance, and ineptitude.

I began to frequent the Peabody Book Store and Beer Stube, a Baltimore landmark a few blocks from my apartment, once patronized by the curmudgeonly author and critic H. L. Mencken among other Baltimore icons. Its front room, down a few steps from Charles Street, was littered with old books, its old walls with posters and paintings and other detritus of the years. In the back were wood tables where, over a beer and sandwich, you could sit and watch the Great Dantini, a magnificently incompetent magician, go through his act. Much later, I'd write about the Peabody, now cruelly demolished. But my selection of it as subject was piqued less by its lore, I think, than by what it meant to me during my early months in town.

It was through the Peabody that I met Greta. The waitress taking my sandwich and beer order one evening was wearing a distinctive leather vest, all fringes and flourishes; I liked it, told her so, asked her about it. Turns out, her friend Greta had made it for her. Did she think Greta could make me a suede sport jacket? I left with Greta's phone number and called her. Greta said sure. We arranged to meet. I scrawled the details in my datebook: "Meet Greta Kohl at 5:30 pm—Hutzler's Men's Dept, Howard near Lexington," in the middle of the city's still vibrant downtown shopping district. She quoted me $55, including $20 for the suede itself—like maybe three or four hundred today. A few days later I went up to her place in Harford County so she could measure me for it.

Greta lived out in the country, in a tiny stone cottage that looked like it went back to the Revolution, situated on a dirt road, untouched by sprawl, untouched by anything, really. Greta was an artist, an oil painter, seven years older than I, tall, lovely to behold, with thick brown hair cut close, severely even, and a sculptured face that belonged on Mount Rushmore. She was completely serious, smiled rarely; like Gary Cooper, at least in his Hollywood persona, she had little to say, often not much more than a *yup* or a *nope*. But when she draped the soft brown suede across my shoulders and back, I felt her hands and not the leather.

Greta came round once to my apartment for a fitting and then, about two weeks later—this was by now mid-October—the job was done and we arranged to celebrate, meeting at a restaurant in Baltimore's Little Italy for dinner. The jacket fit perfectly. Her work was beautiful. The buttons were fashioned from pieces of thicker leather. The inside breast pocket bore a suede patch on which she'd inked, in her brusque and utilitarian way, "Constructed by G. Kohl." We had drinks, we ate, and, across the softly lit table, we talked—not lightly, not easily, but we talked—probably about her plans to join the Peace Corps. And then, at a pause in our sometimes labored conversation, she looked up at me and, out of nowhere, declared her wish to sleep with me. She explained, with a sly little smile that, set against her usual seriousness, was bewitching, "I like living out in the country. But it gets cold. I need a warm body, too."

We drove separately to my apartment. Me in the dilapidated Peugeot I still had from college, she in her old Jeep. This was when Jeeps were still Jeeps, bare, functional tools; but for years after that evening, until they were all tarted up and ubiquitous, Jeeps to me were sexy. Greta and I made love. We fell asleep. At some point in the early morning, I felt a rustling. It was Greta, beside me, getting up. I looked up in confusion and alarm: Why did she need to go? Oh, she had to get started on the long drive back to Harford County. "Gotta feed the chickens," she said. And she was gone.

Soon, our relationship was reduced to letters, first from her Peace Corps training camp in New Mexico, then from Guatemala, where she'd write me of the civil war there and her efforts on behalf of the villagers. Before she left, though, we got together a few more times. Once, I stayed over at her stone cottage in the country. It felt like a doll's house, with its narrow staircase leading to her bedroom, her bed all quilts and fabrics, everywhere paintings, color.

The place was warm with her artistic energy and her breed of Spartan femininity, but otherwise, that next autumn morning, cold. We huddled under the covers, but then, eventually, I had to get up and go. It was already too late to drive into the city, shower and dress for work at home, then turn around and drive back the other way to my job. So finally I just jumped out of bed and, scarcely washing up, threw on my clothes and drove straight to work. Soon after I got in, I went to the lavatory. I stood over the urinal, the intoxicating aroma of the night's lovemaking wafting up to me. There, in that instant, was my Baltimore life, my young manhood, my growing up. I was happy.

⌣‾

Six months into Baltimore, I got a new car. With a little help from my dad, I was making enough at my job to ditch the Peugeot and buy a sports car, of a breed certified to earn the eternal love of women. Mine was an English runabout a few years old, a Triumph Spitfire convertible, in bright lemon-yellow, nothing shy and retiring about it. Life out of school, it was starting to seem, was goodies and surprises, pleasures and thrills.

And the thing is, I knew it. I didn't take it for granted. I realized that life had turned sweet on me.

Paradoxically, my delight during these heady months lay not in their novelty and freshness but in what I understood as their normality; all this, I imagined, was what everyone else had been doing *all along*, and now, at last, I was, too. I wasn't thinking much about the war; it was easy to be heedless of the world's troubles. I was young. I was on my own for the first time. My life was my life, I wanted it to be interesting, and it was. I was no celebrity, diplomat, test pilot or scientist. But I had a good life, with ordinary friends, indulging in ordinary pleasures, all financed by a good, steady job – though the job itself, as I'll explain at the proper time, was not quite "ordinary."

There was nothing so unusual about the

experiences that first year bestowed on me—nothing except that I said yes to them. That was new.

3

Brooklyn, about 1955.

I was eight or nine, in the school gym, lingering beside the basketball court; I don't remember what brought me there. I do remember the wood floors, the walls of hard ceramic tile in beige or muted yellow; the boys and the bobble of the ball and the scuffling feet, bursts of sound and movement, hard breathing, the deep, hollow sound of the ball dribbled and passed, the boys in a blur of movement.

Then a halt, almost a silence, as they gathered, taking their positions for the next play, then another chorus of sound and movement.

They weren't much bigger than I, maybe a year or two older. They played. I watched, off to the side, transfixed, observing out of the corner of my eye. Another flurry of action, another halt, another second or two of near-quiet. But this time the moment's silence was broken, as one boy, chin up toward me, looked over and asked, "Hey, you wanna play?"

"Nah, that's awright."

That was all. But *of course* I wanted to play. *Of course* I wanted to join the other boys and give myself over to their play. Anybody would. I did. But I said no. Reflexively. Out of something like smallness, or timidity—to be followed by a lifetime of shame, a word I use here with some care and exactitude.

I could have offered every sort of reason, to myself or anyone bothering to ask, for why I said no: I didn't know how to play basketball, so how could I play? Basketball wasn't my sport, baseball was. I played stickball and punchball, and others of baseball's myriad offshoots on the streets and sandlots near my house. Baseball, and the Brooklyn Dodgers, was me. What was basketball, this alien thing? What did I know about basketball? I didn't know the teams, didn't know the rules. Besides, whatever had brought me to the gym that day, I had to get home, right?

These "reasons," of course, amounted to nothing compared to my deep wanting, to be on the court with the other boys, the big ball bounding, the scuffling and the driving, the shot arcing toward the hoop. The truth is, I said "No," when every part of me wanted to say "yes." It would have taken just a few steps from the sidelines to the knot of boys on the court, a few moments of confusion and uncertainty, of feeling foolish and inept, and then, who knows? But I couldn't move. And once I said "no" that day, it was if "no" became embedded in my DNA. I played no basketball that day, nor later, never in high school, never in college. Never learned the rules. Never dribbled. Never jumped. Never drove toward the basket. Never. Not once.

As child, adolescent, and teenager, I did my share of stupid, hurtful things. One time we were rehearsing a school play about the Pilgrims, maybe second or third grade, and Margaret was being silly, so I slapped her, just because I couldn't stand her stupid giggling. Another time, I fired my slingshot at some kid I didn't even know, just to do it—I held no particular grudge against him—and hit him, hurt him; a few days later, his friends waylaid me after Hebrew school and beat the shit out of me. At my bar mitzvah, when the rabbi launched into a disquisition on the spiritual "costs" of insufficiently Jewish behavior and presented me with a bible, the insufferable twerp I was piped up for all to hear, "Awright, so how much does it cost?"

There were lots more times like these but, in the ordinary run of adolescent male pathology, they were mostly as predictable and uninteresting. They were awful, sure, causing me or my parents trouble and embarrassment, but I haven't stewed over them much. I cite them here, but they don't gnaw at me the way the basketball court does, or Don's.

Don's was a little candy store on Avenue M a few blocks from the house, just off the street I took to school every day. Don's was the place to be. But if you ask why, I couldn't have told you then and can't tell you now, because I never went in. We had a similar store closer to the house, across Utica Avenue, which I did go into sometimes, for an egg cream, or to fetch a newspaper or pack of cigarettes for my mother. As an eight- or ten-year-old, I didn't feel entirely comfortable going in there either. But the front of it, with big windows, right on the corner, was open and "public"—better than the back, where the older boys hung out, secreted away among themselves, their realm. Don's must have been something like this, but I can't really say. It was just *Don's*, its very name bearing a cachet that somehow kept me at a distance. I never went in. I didn't challenge my fear. I didn't set it as a goal to overcome. I just surrendered.

My Brooklyn was not the urgent, bustling Brooklyn Alfred Kazin immortalized in *A Walker in the City,* or Spike Lee's Bed-Stuy, but a corner of the outer borough built up mostly after the war, less dense, diverse, and interesting. The trolley car tracks connecting the neighborhood to downtown Brooklyn had been ripped up and replaced by buses in the year or two after my grandparents, upstairs, and my parents, downstairs, moved there in 1948. The subway didn't reach this far; later, to get to high school in Manhattan, I had to take a bus to connect with it.

Our neighborhood was a step up for working- and middle-class people and small businessmen, mostly Jewish, Italian, and some Irish, largely products of the tenements, apartment buildings, and row houses of Brooklyn's older precincts. My father had been born on the Lower East Side, the son of

Yiddish-speaking immigrants from eastern Europe, but grew up in Brooklyn. My mother's father was from the old country, too, but her mother was born in New York. Dad ran a small metal-finishing business at the other end of the borough. Our next door neighbor drove a cab. Frankie's dad was a printer, Lawrence's was a butcher, Lee's a photographer, Mike's a baker. Mothers mostly stayed home.

Growing up, I shared a bedroom with my brother Harry. He was seven years younger than I, so when I was in sixth grade at P.S. 203 he was still little. The one desk in our room, a hollow-core door spanning the gap between our two painted pine dressers, was mine for schoolwork. From my perch there, I could look out across the garden, over the thick hedge that separated it from the Flatlands Avenue traffic.

That broad street was laid out at a sharp angle to the grid of brick rowhouses, blocks and blocks of them, that made up most of our neighborhood. Wherever it cut into the regular street grid, it left a wedge too small to build on but big enough for a sandlot or garden. Ours was a garden my grandfather lovingly tended, with a crabapple tree, a trellis of roses, and small landscaped islands set on the triangular patch of lawn, bordered by hedges. That was nice for him and sometimes for us in the summer when the mosquitos weren't too bad.

But by slicing into the grid where it did, Flatlands Avenue cut off our street, East 51st, making it skimpily short, just six narrow houses in length. On the other side of Flatlands, it became a long, lovely, tree-shaded stretch of close-packed houses, with plenty of families, plenty of kids. Ours, by contrast, was a stub, like a finger lopped off in an industrial accident. The front of our house looked out on that little stump. The back abutted a gas station. One long side of the house we shared with our neighbors, the Feldmans. The other faced Flatlands, where the sidewalk was too narrow, the street too wide, and nothing ever happened except for cars whizzing by. No boy's land.

So when I think of "the neighborhood," I think of our block with its scant crop of kids, set against the activity and hidden pleasures of the long, cozy blocks adjacent to it. I came to think that this quirk of geography made a difference to me growing up. I suppose I *needed* it to make a difference, so it could shoulder the blame for how I felt cut off, forever at the edge. But this feels thin to me now. I don't buy it any more. I mean, Frankie Russo, just two houses over, managed just fine.

At the time I was, say, ten, Frankie was 12 or 13. He lived with his parents and sister in one of four connected houses, just past the Feldmans, that were a little older and a little smaller than ours. Theirs was Italian Catholic Brooklyn, built around the local church, Mary Queen of Heaven, alien and exotic to us. Frankie was short, dark, wiry and muscular.

In those postwar years, a few parked cars lined the street and occasionally one of them moved; but not many and not often, so we could play punchball or stickball on the street.

Home plate, a steel sewer-cover embedded in the asphalt, lay roughly in front of our house; the "field" was the short stretch of street that extended to Avenue K, six houses down. When Frankie stood at the plate and punched a pink Spaldeen or swung a broom-handled bat, he was all grace, his facial features untroubled, his movements liquid and relaxed. But it wasn't his athletic prowess alone that lands him among my yearnings and regrets, it was how he stood at the center of things, exhibiting a quiet magnetism that drew others to him. He wasn't just Frankie, but Frankie-and-his-friends—Arnie, and Pinhead, and others whose names I never knew. Frankie was always with his friends. And they were always with him, on the street or crowded onto his family's little brick porch.

Like Frankie, I played stickball and punchball, or softball in a nearby lot among different constellations of boys. Once, at bat, I broke my wrist teetering back from a ball that would have hit me and falling hard into the dirt; I got a thick plaster cast for it and, a few days later, Mrs. Moskowitz from East 52nd phoned my mother to say I was using it as a stickball bat. We played five boxes, a sidewalk game in which you bounced a ball into one sidewalk square, then, in successive turns, and with greater difficulty, two, all the way up to five; or skelly, down on your knees, shooting bottlecaps across a field chalked in the street.

My friends, from the neighborhood, from school, from the Boy Scouts, included Lawrence at the end of the block, Lainie Feldman from next door, Lee on Schenectady Avenue, Robert and Stu across Flatlands, Sheila on East 52nd, Barry and Jerry on Avenue K, and later Clyde on East 46th. I recite these names as if they were badges of social inclusion. As if, clumped into the paragraph together, they belonged together, one happy family of friends of which I was part.

But it wasn't that way. Mostly, my friends didn't know one another. Except in the Boy Scouts, which I joined at my friend Michael's urging when I was 11, I almost never got together with groups of the same boys. More often it was me and each of them, alone, or with random neighborhood kids I didn't know at all. Playing ball in Lawrence's driveway, just the two of us, desultorily hitting the ball over Arlene's roof; or playing Monopoly with Lee in my room, just the two of us. My childhood and adolescence on East 51st Street reached across 14 years, in one house, on one block. But the events culled from those years make no thick, flavorful stew of memories but only a thin, watery soup. I belonged to no group, community, clique, or set. Certainly not to Frankie-and-his-friends.

I was an intelligent boy. But I never applied what intelligence I had to my loneliness, which is what it was. I didn't *get* groups; they baffled me, their social force fields impossible to navigate. And it didn't take much of a group to fluster me; *three* was quite enough. Attention to one person meant lack of attention to another and, with it, the awful certainty that I was missing something—a look, a nod, a snigger, anything, everything. Automatically—as at the basketball court that day, or at the thought of stepping into the social maelstrom of Don's candy store—I'd withdraw, close myself down, say no. Say no, even as I wanted to say yes, wanted to be stitched into something bigger. Years ago, I wrote a long magazine article about the lives of laboratory rats. As part of my research I made it my business to be on hand when the carton in which they were shipped arrived at the lab. As the technician opened it and they were exposed to the light, the baby rats squirmed and slithered all together, pink and trembling, a single living organism. I envied them.

In my room as a child, I was exquisitely aware that something was going on, or might be going on, just outside on the street. It was a matter merely of leaving my room, a few steps through the living room, a few more down the hall, and out the door onto East 51st. But too often, I never got there. Outside my bedroom door were Mom and Dad. Our living room was closed off from the promise of the street by heavy drapes, often shut tight. Boundaries. Barriers. The real blockage, of course, was me: Always I felt a tension between inside, where I felt constrained to remain, and outside, which was tugging at me. I feel something of this same tension even today.

Today, if my wife, or a friend, or the TV weather-person turns bleak and glum at the specter of even a light spring shower, I shake my head in gentle derision at what strikes me as a kneejerk reaction. I've always loved rain. A drizzle, a downpour—doesn't much matter. I enjoy the freshness of it against my skin, the way it heightens my senses. These, anyway, are the reasons I give. And they are true. But they are not all of it. After a violent squall, I *watch* myself grow anxious as the patter of the raindrops lessens. My response is so extreme—so persistent, so at odds with others—that there *must* be more to it. Maybe it's this: As a child, rain eased the tension between outside and inside. If it was nice out, Frankie Russo and the street's possibilities beckoned, forever in conflict with whatever I was supposed to be doing at home. But if it was raining, I *couldn't* go out: I was inside, and that was that, and it was easy, and my discomfort dissipated, and everything was fine.

But just what, so insistently, drew me inside?

"If I don't know, your father knows. And if your

father doesn't know, I know. And if neither of us know," my mother would add in a way supposed to sound amusing or ironic but actually sounded like she meant it, "it's not worth knowing." I grew up absorbing the idea, and half believing it, that there was a *sufficiency* at home, that all I needed I'd find right there, with them. My mother and father were both college grads. They read incessantly, fiction and nonfiction, in subjects literary, technical, historical, and intellectual. They talked with me about science, about business, about Jewish culture, about Shakespeare, poetry, the Broadway stage, language, Rex Stout and Rex Harrison, Wordsworth and Keats.

But never flatly, never for the sake of raw knowledge or bare fact.

In the living room of our apartment hung a small framed print of a Winslow Homer painting: three great palm trees, silhouetted against storm clouds, their fronds gathered up by the wind, the sea disturbed. For all we know, the storm inspiring Homer's 1898 painting missed the little island cottages in the foreground, leaving them untouched. But *Bahama Hurricane* is no demure landscape; it celebrates all the power of the still distant storm, its black, roiling energy. Years later, I saw it again, on a museum card, and abruptly it restored me to childhood: Drama and high feeling legitimized, made the stuff of the everyday—this, I think, summed up one strain of our family life, for my mother and father alike, each in their own ways.

For my mother, everything was a Shakespearean sonnet, or a high-kicking Broadway musical, or a lost civilization, or the thick fog of an English murder mystery, or a family story heavy with drama. Growing up, the stories she told me were not necessarily—almost never, really—children's stories. No vapid heroes or brave little boys for Bea Kanigel. She didn't read me fairy tales, fables, or Winnie the Pooh. She did read to me of thieves and outlaws. Like Howard Pyle's Robin Hood. And Alfred Noyes's "The Highwayman." *The road was a ribbon of moonlight over the purple moor.* Or Edgar Alan Poe's "The Purloined Letter," with all its delight at the guilty letter left in plain view, evading the eyes of the police.

She was a wonderful writer herself. Letters she wrote me later were never merely informative; she didn't much bother with news. She'd transfigure ordinary travel accounts into adventures, invariably spiced with a line or two from Shakespeare. Later, she wrote and had published several reminiscences, like one about her grandmother:

> Sometimes a trick of the light as the sun goes down recalls a walk we took together. A bit of fabric glimpsed in a store window, a taste of yeast cake, the sight of the crabapples on the tree outside my window, burnished and russet in the autumn sun, all bring the memories

stirring out of the past. I feel again her warm, dry hand in mine like a blessing on the day.

Another time she wrote about playing Guinevere in a version of the Broadway musical *Camelot* that her Jewish women's group put on. At the last minute, she had to fill in for her friend Elaine, who was "five-foot-eight, lushly contoured and blessed with a bosom of Wagnerian splendor," which her own, she thought, was not. So Elaine's Guinevere costume needed surgery:

> Everyone in the cast who admitted to a padded bra rallied round the flagging bust line. We stuffed in everything we could find, but nothing would close the gap. Never have so many done so much for so little. The bodice that on Elaine surged proudly forward on me simply drooped.

All my mother said or did she did with attitude and style; she couldn't do it any other way, didn't know how. When we played Scrabble, the game was never a matter of passing the time, of just setting down words and toting up scores; there was *blood* in it. When she'd score a "whole word," using all seven letters from her rack (a "bingo" to the rest of the world), she'd lay them down, one by one, deliberately, ceremoniously, like a lawyer setting out his brief or a duelist laying out his pistol.

I came to think later that my mother was never entirely of this world. She'd never quite transcended her first great joy, her four years at Brooklyn College as an English major, in the late 1930s. Her head was forever awhirl in the English romantic poets, but also in archaeology, in anthropology—in the past; in Depression-era movies of twenty years before, in her childhood in Brooklyn's Bushwick neighborhood, her beloved grandmother just next door.

Of course, as a 1950s wife and mother, she managed. She shopped with her mother on Fulton Street in downtown Brooklyn, prepared meals, washed clothes, packed for our vacations. But I never felt that the indifferent trifles of daily life mattered much to her. More so even than my father, she inhabited another, prior world more than this one— one painted in sepia and sprinkled with sequins.

For her eighteenth birthday in 1939, three years before their marriage, my father gave my mom a one-volume edition of Thomas Mann's novel, *The Magic Mountain.* "From Charles," he wrote on the inside cover, "With sincerest wishes for a whole flock of happy birthdays." The blue cloth-bound book, published by Knopf, the famous borzois on the title page, became a kind of sacred relic in the house. Periodically, they'd talk of the Swiss sanitarium to which Hans Castorp went for three weeks, only to remain for seven years; of Settembrini, the humanist; of Naphta, a Jew who had turned into a cruel, fascistic Jesuit. Here was intellectual combat glorified, impassioned debates held up as normal, worthy, and apt. I would not read *The Magic Mountain* myself until after I got to Baltimore, where one afternoon I commandeered a table in a coffee shop off Mt. Vernon Place and consumed its last hundred pages—at last a Kanigel in good standing!

During my growing-up years, my father ran a small electroplating shop on the second floor of an old loft building across the street from the Brooklyn Navy Yard. After suffering several business failures, my mother's father had started it in the 1920s, and now my dad owned a piece of it, Egyptian Polishing and Plating Works by name. Steaming chemical vapors hung over great open tanks of pickling and plating solutions. Powerful muscled men, wearing black, thigh-high rubber boots and rubber gauntlets, carried copper bars of wire-linked record racks, or Clairol display racks, from tank to tank. The place was metal-flecked, filthy, poisoned with toxic cyanide solutions, but for me, growing up, it was a place of high drama.

"We Kanigels," my father liked to say, "have cyanide in our blood." Sometimes on weekday mornings, Dad, on the way into the shop, would save me the bus ride to the subway stop at Eastern Parkway and drive me there instead. Along the way he'd ply me with accounts of the men who worked for him, their merits, failings and peculiarities; of the company delivery truck getting stuck in the tangled streets of lower Manhattan; of the union threatening a strike or the most recent theft of nickel anodes. Here was his hiring philosophy: If a man walked in off the street looking for a job, he'd say, "Come back tomorrow." If he did, he'd passed the first test and had a shot at a job.

Each day, my father's work took him into "the jungle," as he called it, where business suddenly dried up, customers didn't pay, tanks leaked, and faithful but hard-drinking employees had to be bailed out of jail. He was proud of his ability to inhabit the big, bad world. Yet right alongside Egyptian's business kinks and catastrophes, he inhabited whole other mental universes that, in his telling, were to me just as dramatic and alive. He talked of Cooper Union, the elite, free-tuition engineering school he'd attended in the 1930s; of the aircraft carrier catapults his friend Morris designed; of the Michelson-Morley experiment of the 1880s that anticipated Einstein's theory of relativity; of the sheer *chutzpah* of the Russian mathematician Lobachevski daring to imagine parallel lines, which by definition never meet, meeting.

In the 1950s, the wartime destruction of European Jewry was not long past and my parents didn't shrink from discussing it, or viewing the awful documentaries of the concentration camps, with their stick-like survivors, or the death camps with their stacks of corpses. My father, who came from an Orthodox family but was no longer observant, told me how the Jews of Europe went to the gas chambers with the words of the *Shema,* Judaism's bedrock prayer, on their lips; the Nazis had killed his mother's brother and two of her sisters, I learned later. It was impossible, he declared, to be a pacifist in World War II. "It was only the force of Allied arms," he said often enough that I could never forget it, and in exactly those words, that had stopped Hitler from killing all the Jews, everywhere. My father confronted these cruel facts, drove them into my head, deemed it his responsibility to do so, summoning every resource of urgency he could command.

Their personalities were so different, my mother and father, she mannered and theatrical, he intense and emphatic, but in this one respect they were alike—that they left you thinking that life, even in the everyday interstices that took up most of it, wasn't to be thought of as flat, placid, or routine; that nothing so quotidian as a paycheck, or painting a room, or social chatter were really what counted; that literature, the call of history, poetry, wordplay and the mysteries of language, the drama of human achievement and human failure, the life of the mind, were not schoolbook trifles, but the *real* business of life. It's only slight exaggeration to say that never was a word spoken or story told in our house for the sake of raw information alone; everything carried an electric charge of meaning.

For my first seven years I was an only child and even after my brother came along, and then, the year before I went off to college, my sister Rachele, I looked to my parents more than to friends. They must have figured they were all I really needed and in many ways they were. Certainly they took great, lively interest in my schoolwork, in my papers and projects, in whatever I was studying or reading. Dad brought home plastic tubs, lengths of copper wire and plating solutions to help me with a science project. Mom oversaw my paper on the life of Broadway. I hung out with them, absorbing their interests and habits of mind. I remember thinking after I was out of college that, all through the four years, I'd never met anyone half as interesting as they.

So it was a good place, our little house. But it was my parents' show. They were formidable people, Mom and Dad, and I was a boy. Set against the intensity they brought to everything, I sometimes felt diminished and small, gently squeezed into a comfortable box. They spoke, I mostly listened, usually with unfeigned focus and interest; my parents didn't blab or babble. They found in me a worthy audience, one for whom they could perform, someone they could intrigue with their ideas, memories, speeches and stories, all that made them fascinating in their own eyes, and fascinating in mine. They must have enjoyed and appreciated my ready receptivity, how I'd listen raptly to their every word, my eyes on theirs, undistracted, *still.*

The first time I wrote that last sentence, I was on vacation with my wife at an Appalachian Mountain Club camp on Lake Winnipesaukee in New Hampshire. It wasn't a working vacation, but on some days I found myself in the cabin or by the dock recording vagrant memories, taking notes, writing in pencil about some of the incidents and themes of this book, especially about my childhood. And with "...eyes on theirs, undistracted, *still,*" my pencil wavered. At that last word, it hovered over the paper in momentary incapacity, for fifteen or twenty seconds, unable to commit, to *still* with its air of easy receptivity, or *stilled*—as in tamped down, subdued, silenced.

It was one of the few times I'd felt, in so abrupt and visceral a way, the ambivalence I'd felt as a boy—between, on the one hand, respect and love for my parents, and, on the other, a dusky resentment: In the shadow of their fluency and intellect, under their benign thumb, I sometimes felt passive, timid, too acutely attuned to their interests, not enough to my own.

For many years, I would assert to myself, as indisputable fact, that my parents and I talked about everything. It was not true. We did not. I don't recall outright taboos. But my parents couldn't be interested in everything, and their universe contained vast emptinesses that, because I was so close to them, the oldest son, in whom they invested so much, I didn't

see—areas of life they didn't talk about, or participate in, or encourage, because they weren't much
interested themselves.

I don't remember either of them ever saying,
"Rob, you ought to get out more and see your
friends." Spending hours in my room, reading, I was
not encouraged to go out and play. Friends, and the
world of clubs, teams and groups, were secondary
or irrelevant. It was left to me to figure out how to
fit in, or, really, what it *meant* to fit in. The idea of
"being accepted," or the other formulas one hears
on behalf of a healthy social life, never surfaced in
our house; the weight, the attention, was elsewhere.
The everyday social rituals and intrigues that grease
the workings of the world were *terra incognito* to me.
When I was 13 or 14 and developed serial crushes on
girls, I couldn't have told you what a crush was, or
meant; I'm not sure I knew the word.

I never heard my parents discuss what it meant to
look good, or why you'd want to; dressing up meant
wearing the right category of shirt, tie, or jacket for
the occasion. That was it. I never learned to pick out
clothes, or look to what others wore, or observe which
colors went with which, or what it meant for colors
to "match" in the first place; this was true in elementary, junior high, and high school equally. My dad
sometimes got me clothes at an army surplus store,
and one winter my go-to outerwear was an olive drab
jacket probably last worn by a GI in Korea; I liked it

fine. But Jon, a junior high classmate I didn't like, mocked me for it; he always wore a snappy dress shirt and neatly creased slacks. So when he failed an algebra test and Mr. Saikin publicly chided him, I relished the moment—Jon's impeccable wardrobe and mathematical ineptness revealed as two sides of the same miserable human being.

Once, in the car, inching through the Lower East Side, my dad acknowledged the Puerto Ricans we saw around us on the old Jewish streets: "They live in slums, tenements, a lot of them, but once they step out on the street, well, look at them..."—men and women, beautiful, dressed in lively colors, stylish. They'd worked at it, of course, and I don't think he quite understood that. To my dad—who always looked pretty rough around the edges, shirt pulled out from around his short barrel waist, the jacket and tie he wore to work often stained by chemicals—all this style and fashion splendor was a wonder, almost a new idea. As for my mom, like most middle-class Jewish women, she tried to look her best. But somehow, that idea never got to me: Maybe I looked OK, maybe I didn't, but, either way, it wasn't something to think about.

My parents didn't dismiss sports and athleticism as unworthy; but such things didn't *matter* to them. They bought me a tricycle, promptly stolen, and a bike, which I learned to ride at age 11. Sometimes I'd tool around Marine Park, once or twice riding over the bridge at the end of Flatbush Avenue to Riis Park. I played ball. I followed the Dodgers; my father, though a Giants fan, didn't dare say anything against Duke Snider, Gil Hodges, and the other boys of summer, gods to me and every other worthy Brooklynite. The few times I remember having a catch with him in front of the house, his throws and catches were energetic, but twitchy and awkward. Even the ping pong we sometimes played in our unfinished basement seemed to him, I think, an intellectual exercise, a game of strategy and smarts, not the work of the body. My mother, I liked to joke later, was an avid mountaineer, by which I meant that she loved *reading* about Himalayan mountain climbing expeditions. She knew all the lore of Annapurna and Everest. One morning in 1953 she woke me up with the news that Hillary and Tenzing had reached Everest's summit. But as for so much as going for a walk, much less a serious hike, either around the neighborhood or in the country, I don't remember her doing that, or riding a bike, or exercising at all.

The only realm worthy of real encouragement in our house was that of books, of the intellect, of arts and ideas and the big world; it was impossible to read too much in our house. And I didn't fight it. In kindergarten and first grade I'd followed an ordinary enough path, making friends with Billy Max, Joe Lietto, and other neighborhood boys. But in third grade, I was uprooted in the middle of the year from

Mrs. Light's third grade class and plopped into Mrs. Dolley's fourth grade; I'd been "skipped," which owed to my parents, who thought I should be moving along faster through school, as they both had, and had lobbied for it with the principal. A triumph it was made to seem around the house. My mom wrote me a celebratory note, quoting a line from Tennyson's poem "Ulysses": "To strive, to seek, to find, and not to yield."

When it was time for junior high school, which back then covered the 7th and 8th grade together with the first year of high school, I was admitted to the SP program, for "Special Progress," where you'd do the three years in two. Then, when I was still 12, I took the exam for admission to the special high schools of New York City. I was admitted to one of them, Stuyvesant, which would take me out of the neighborhood altogether—an hour and twenty minutes each day on the bus and subway into Manhattan for the next three years.

I don't remember being asked whether I wanted to skip a grade, or do SP, or attend Stuyvesant. I don't remember thinking one way or the other about them, don't remember any of them as a choice. They just happened. I took them as they came, unquestioning, uncomplaining. Even now, in retrospect, I don't think they were so terribly bad for me. I got a jump academically. I wasn't miserable being thrust into Mrs. Dolley's class, or in SP, and certainly not at

Stuyvesant, which was a wonder of a place.

But they took a toll. Being skipped into the fourth grade helped edge me toward ambition and personal achievement, at the expense of neighborhood friends my own age. Same thing in junior high, where none of my P.S. 203 classmates were with me in SP, and where again I knew no one. Likewise at Stuyvesant, its students, pulled from all the five boroughs, none of them known to me before that September day in 1959 when we all stood, lined up outside the hulking gray edifice of the school on East 15th Street, waiting to enter for the first time.

One day when I was 13 or 14, at the end of one of those long commutes back to Brooklyn, I got off the bus and, approaching my block, realized something had changed: I was set off from the neighborhood and most of my friends from East 51st Street, and just then I knew it. I had, ostensibly, done a great thing: I was two years ahead. I was in the best high school in the city, reveling in its pressure-cooker academic atmosphere, with wonderful teachers, me and most of my classmates bound for good colleges. I stood apart, which is supposed to be a good thing.

But where were Frankie Russo and his friends? Where had they gone?

Of course, it was I who had gone.

By now, though, a new tape had begun to play in my head, one that quietly warred with all I'd absorbed at home and that would lead me soon to college and career. It had been laid down the summer before I enrolled at Stuyvesant.

For four summers, ages 9 to 13, I'd gone to summer camp for two-week stretches. The first two were at Pioneer Youth Camp in upstate New York, with its socialist-lite flavor, where counselors would break into choruses of "Solidarity Forever," the old workers' song. The next two were at a Boy Scout camp not far away. I have pleasant, if fuzzy, memories of these entirely conventional summers—of tents mounted atop wooden platforms, of the woods and open air, of swimming and campfires. But they neither sped me toward, nor retarded me from, becoming the person I seemed bent on becoming.

On the final day of that fourth summer, my folks picked me up at Boy Scout camp in Narrowsburg, NY, and drove me to where they were staying on their vacation. It was a farm house set along a dirt road at the base of a mountain ridge. It had rooms for about a dozen guests, who'd gather in the homey downstairs dining room around long tables for meals. It was called City Slicker Farm and was run by a middle-aged German-American couple, Eva and Kurt. Much of the work of serving meals, washing dishes and tidying up rooms was entrusted to their golden-haired teenaged daughters and their friends from back in northern New Jersey, where they lived the rest of the year, and with each of whom, one after the other, I fell in love.

Eva and Kurt, who had immigrated in the 1920s, spoke with soft German accents that, thanks to their leftwing leanings and impeccable personal histories, to me bore none of the Nazi taint things German held for me; they were all sweetness, decency and healthy *Gemütlichkeit*. Kurt, eager and ebullient, was a skilled machinist who'd pelt me with math problems and talk about science. He played the flute, played chess and square-danced, too. Eva was the matriarch, in the kitchen with its old-fashioned coal stove, presiding over the whole operation with wizened humor and quiet authority.

I fell in with their beautiful daughters—Bette, 17 that first year, bound for college in the fall, and Cathy, 15, and Cathy's dark-tressed friend, Jan. Those two golden summers collapse into one, a riot of blond hair and long tanned legs, of joking, teasing, and song; it took nothing, barely a word or a look, for Cathy, with her guitar, and Jan to break into song.

Along country roads canopied with trees, we'd hike into town. I was the son of paying guests (normally targets of derisive jesting among them), but mostly I felt part of the gang. Just up the hill from the main house was the barn, with a rickety, unpainted room where, that second summer, Jan and Cathy slept. Sometimes, after dark, I'd troop up there and join them, there enjoying my first tastes of sexual play, innocent and incomplete. At summer's end and for the next few years, I wrote to all of them. Back in Brooklyn, I'd wait for the clunk of the heavy brass mail slot that might mean a letter or card from one of them. I'd study their light and inconsequential missives for what they thought about me, always in frank wonder at their school clubs and Christmases and skiing and boys and girls together, their leafy suburban lives alluringly alien.

From the beginning, and in the years after, and ever since, those two summers filled my heart and fancy. Later, I tried to figure out just why, but I never got much beyond the obvious—the simple fact that I was deliciously happy at feeling part of something so fresh and different from anything I'd known. At a time when I was gritting my teeth for the promised rigors of Stuyvesant and later college, the farm offered a counter narrative. City Slicker—the girls, their friends, the group I had become a small part of, the house itself with the hill rising high behind it, that good family, those evenings full of music—left me with a taste for "normal" unfraught happiness that didn't demand achievement and struggle.

<hr />

In June 1962, I graduated from high school and in September enrolled at Rensselaer Polytechnic

Institute, an engineering school in Troy, New York, where for four years I was surrounded by smart, capable students mostly devoid of genius or style. Most were careerist, conventional, and hard-working, as was I. A hundred and fifty miles up the Hudson Valley out of the city, I encountered anti-Semitism— often from guys I *liked*, actually—but also, to my wonder and incomprehension, anti-Catholicism. Fred, from a little town in upstate New York, took me aside one day to whisper about a student from across the hall, a likeable Italian-American fellow named Joe. He was *Catholic*. He owed allegiance to the *Pope*. He was religiously misguided, malevolent. On he went, with creepy, conspiratorial bitterness. But Fred, I said, he's *Christian*, isn't he?

Small-town RPI was fraternities, beer-drinking, hockey and hard work into the night, tooling away on problem sets. I did well enough in English and history, but struggled through differential equations and solid mechanics, with its intimidating tensor analysis, and some of the other tough courses— and some that weren't so much tough as tedious. Rensselaer, the oldest engineering school in the country, was supposed to be a good school, and I suppose it was. But not for me. And poor browbeaten Troy, cast down from its former heights as collar-maker to the world, was no place to grow up.

I was scarcely 16 when my dad drove me up there and deposited me in my dorm. As a freshman, I dug in, trying to make my way, and did OK. In sophomore year, I was miserable, lost, and fat. In my junior year, I was active in the fencing club, where I made some friends, traveled to other local schools for tournaments, and enjoyed wisps of a recognizable college experience. Senior year I was thinking about nothing so much as getting out and what I'd do next. Some of my classmates were going into the navy, others landing jobs in industry. But several guys I admired seemed bent on graduate school and, without thinking too hard about it, I figured I'd do the same.

And then the train slipped off the tracks.

It was late fall of 1965, midway through my senior year. Walking to class, I had just come down the long outside stairway between the athletic center and the football field, thinking about post-graduation plans, weighing the merits of this grad program or that. Law, business, and engineering all appealed to me in different ways. A fascinating course in economics and antitrust law had left me ready to break up General Motors—so yes, maybe law. Business? Back in high school, I'd had an adolescent fling with Ayn Rand and the nutty capitalist heroes of her novel *Atlas Shrugged,* which left me fantasizing about the Kanigel Industries I'd one day launch. And then there was engineering itself—maybe I should pick up a masters before I did anything else. Some of my smarter classmates had seduced me with the wonders of fluid flow, the Navier-Stokes equations, and how altogether awesome they were; so while my head for theory was weak and my mathematical talents modest, engineering remained in the picture. One way or the other, I was going to grad school; I'd taken several nationwide admissions tests and scored high. I had only to choose the field.

And then, abruptly, as I reached the bottom of the athletic center steps and continued on past the Troy Building, a vagrant thought rolled right across my brain, like a tank, or a steam roller, brooking no resistance: *I don't want to go to grad school.* I want to get *out* of school.

I don't know where it came from. But I knew it was true.

It wasn't that, visited by this new, alien idea, the more familiar and prudent part of me tried to quash it, or even just tamp it down with reasoned argument. No, neither brain nor heart offered resistance. It was instant capitulation: I needed to get a life. I would not go to grad school. I would get a job. There was no point in arguing with myself.

Sudden visitation, immediate surrender—a nice story. But couldn't it have come in connection with something meatier and more profound? After all, whether one 19-year-old lost soul went on to graduate school or not didn't much matter. Yet just then, as this new idea came along and swamped the old mental circuits, it *did* matter. It had nothing to do with school or job; it had everything to do with who, or what, I listened to, which in this case was my heart. One way of old, familiar thinking was suddenly overridden by a new way, which wasn't thinking at all, but simply truth.

Obviously, what since Freud we call "unconscious" factors figured in, which being unconscious I couldn't have named. But I listened to them. That was the new thing—a quiet voice speaking from within, begging to be heard, the kind I was used to ignoring. This time I paid it heed. And sure enough, a year later, in the summer of 1966, I was in Baltimore, *not* in grad school, with my great, good job, and a social life, doing fine.

4

And I was Rob Kanigel now, too.

Back in Brooklyn, in school and out, I'd sometimes been Rob, sometimes Bob or Robert, but most often just Kanigel, just as my friends were Kurlander, Rosner, Schaefer, or Schwartz. At Rensselaer, I became Bob before I knew it, and Bob I mostly remained through the four years. But I chafed at the mid-American Bobness of it. And now, in Baltimore, I got rid of it altogether. Adopting "Rob," I wrote my friend Jack about some of my early amorous adventures. From Kissena Boulevard in Queens, Jack was a classmate both from Stuy and Rensselaer, where he was my roommate freshman year and then again senior year, an insouciant prodigy who learned everything without apparent effort and spoke in shards of gruff cynicism. He'd noticed Rob replacing Robert. Wasn't it amazing, he wrote from California, "how the loss of one syllable can turn a staid, studious RPI student into the playboy of the armaments industry?"

So it's time, isn't it, that I said something about my job, the one Jack was talking about, the one that had brought me down to Baltimore. It was all about guns. Or really, ammunition. I worked in a room full of drafting tables, about a dozen of them, one of them my own. From this perch, my job was to make better bullets. My job was not to track shipments of them; or to write computer programs collecting data on them; or to run quality control tests on them— nothing so removed, remote or abstract as that. It was the bullet itself I worked on, as a design, a new, more destructive kind intended to tear through the sides of Russian tanks, destroy them, and kill everyone inside. That was my job.

The war in Vietnam was heating up. The North Vietnamese and Viet Cong, our enemies, had Soviet tanks with thick belts of protective armor. Our new ammo, once perfected, would be loaded into the machine guns mounted in American jet fighters and take them out. To improve it was my job and that of the others in the Ammo Lab; this wasn't its real name, but that was the idea—to experiment with, test, refine, and perfect new ammunition.

This one bore the designation "20mm APDS." The twenty millimeter referred to the bore diameter of the rapid-fire cannon from which it was shot, a little more than three-quarters of an inch. The acronym was short for armor-piercing discarding sabot. *Sabot* is a French word for the wooden shoes once worn by French and Belgian peasants; our bullet, propelled by gunpowder exploding within a regular brass cartridge, consisted of a needle-like hard-alloy dart, or flechette, about six inches long, gripped by four miniature plastic shoes; these were the sabots.

The finned flechette looked about like a medieval crossbow bolt. While traveling the length of the cannon barrel, it was gripped by the sabots. But the moment it escaped the barrel, the whole assembly flew apart, the light plastic sabots falling away, the flechette continuing on to its target. There was all sorts of physics to show how this made sense; the pressure within the gun barrel needn't push a load of heavy lead, only the featherweight sabot *carrier* along with the flechette. And the flechette itself could be more aerodynamically shaped. So you'd get higher muzzle velocity, a flatter trajectory, and deliver a more devastating blow to the target. It had been in development for some years, and had been tried earlier, at smaller scale, in rifle ammunition. The Ammo Lab's version was well along in development when I arrived, joining a group intent on making it more reliable, accurate, and deadly.

Early at the Ammo Lab I was assigned to the firing range, located in a quarry at the edge of the company property in an industrial suburb north of the city. Wasn't much, really. A glorified shack set back from the wall of the quarry, with firing stands and electronic instruments, manned by two range officers, guys in their thirties. Bill was the senior man, dark, wavy-haired, serious, and composed. The other, John, looked like Homer Simpson from the later TV cartoon series. When he'd yell *FIRE!*, it came out as *FAHRR!* The range was their domain. They made sure nobody got hurt, that everything was set up right, that all the data were collected, especially that the Polaroid camera properly snapped the oscilloscope trace that recorded pressure inside the gun barrel in the millisecond or so after it was fired.

Our cannon was nothing you could pick up to fire. Whether with conventional rounds or our new ones, it fired projectiles much heavier than any ordinary hunting rifle did; the assembled round with its sabots and flechette, crimped into its brass cartridge, was eight or nine inches long. The long-barreled cannon was set rigidly onto a fixed bed, the test round chambered in its architecture of heavy steel, aimed at a target 100 yards or so downrange, and fired remotely.

When, with due precaution, John finally yelled *FAHRR!*, the cannon boomed, the echo settled, the smoke cleared, and Bill walked me out to the target downrange. There, on a rude steel platform that looked like an overgrown erector set, was clamped a thick armor plate, maybe two feet wide by a foot and a half high, and several inches thick, made from a tough steel alloy, like that used for real tank armor. For each test, it was set at one or another angle to the flight of the flechette, mimicking a battlefield impact.

Soon enough I saw up close what our ammo could do. Most of the time our test projectile penetrated the weighty slab of steel—which to every intuition, every normal human sense of the world, seemed impenetrable; you needn't know its alloy composition or tempering to appreciate its sheer ferrous bulk. Yet now it had a hole through it, black with the heat of the projectile's passage. In the ancient, centuries-long struggle between arms and armor, our flechette had won.

This, anyway, was what I saw from the up-range side of the armor, the front. Now Bill and I circled around a few steps to the back side of the plate, where I could see that the test set-up was more nuanced than I'd supposed. Otherwise unseen, mounted a few inches behind the armor itself, was a thin, seemingly redundant sheet of soft, almost buttery aluminum. But whereas the hole plugged through the armor plate itself was relatively neat, the aluminum behind it was left a big jagged tangle of macerated metal, shredded by the molten-hot steel expelled from the back of the armor.

This flimsy sheet of aluminum was called a witness plate.

Its very softness and vulnerability testified to the mayhem that would be inflicted not on the tank itself but on the crew inside. Part of each test protocol was to describe it and take pictures of the damage. Replaced after each test shot, each sheet of virgin aluminum started out smooth, like the unblemished skin of a boy. Then, in a thousandth of a second, it bore the ugly scars of its traumatic life.

It wasn't as if, in all innocence, I'd simply landed in this world of weaponry. I'd placed myself there, following a path of least resistance that went back to my Uncle George's house in Brooklyn.

George had served in the army in World War II, married my father's sister, and become my dad's close friend. We lived about a ten-minute drive from their house on East 89th Street. When I was in junior high it happened to be an easy walk from school, so I'd sometimes go there for lunch, my Aunt Mini and my grandmother, who lived with them, fawning over me with chicken soup and home-made knishes. One way or another we were at Mini and George's all the time, up the flight of brick steps from the street to their second floor flat. They had a dark, formal living room with a piano, but we never spent any time there. It was always in the modest dinette, off the kitchen, where we'd congregate. Behind it, on the way to the back of the house, was my uncle's manly preserve, his den, with its easy chair, diminutive TV, military magazines, and intriguing *tchotchkes,* like a little brass cannon.

George ran a liquor store in Bedford-Stuyvesant in the years I was growing up. But later he'd do a 180-degree turn from that stressful business, go back to school at nights, pick up a graduate degree, become a physical therapist, and work at increasingly respectable Long Island hospitals, in time moving up to a big house on the Island with my aunt and their two children. I bring this up, years ahead of its proper sequence, because, in retrospect, it was this second career that better represents Uncle George for me: In a medical professional, you want a reassuring certitude. Well, George had that, or conveyed it, anyway. He was a big man with a deep, easy-timbred voice. Long before he gave up the liquor store, while he and Mini were still on East 89th Street, I was drawn to his sure and steadying ways. My dad was an intense, *interesting* man, a bit awkward, geeky, and intellectual; George was a man's man. Later, I'd modify my estimate of him, but back then I was oblivious of his harmless pretensions —he called me "lad," as if he were a Scottish laird—and looked up to him.

In a corner of Uncle George's den stood a tall wood rifle cabinet. I never saw George haul out a pistol, revolver, or other handgun; he had none on display, and I don't know if he owned any. But he kept half a dozen or more rifles and shotguns, standing vertically, all in a row, individually cradled, within his glass-doored cabinet. One or two of them looked like they'd just come from a gunsmith's shop, with tooled wooden stocks, beautifully machined parts, and steel surfaces "blued" to perfection. But more typically they weren't the rare, antique weapons a connoisseur might covet but salt-of-the-earth specimens.

There was an M1 carbine left over from the war.

And a Winchester 94, the classic lever-action rifle with the long tubular magazine under the barrel that boys' BB guns were modeled on. And a Remington semi-automatic shotgun; and a classic bolt-action .30-'06; maybe one or two others. George would take them out and he and my father would take turns making sure their chambers were empty, raising them to their shoulders, sighting along the barrel, and working their "actions"—the cams, catches, and levers that closed around the cartridge, fed it into the firing chamber, and extracted the hot, smoking brass once fired—making steel-slapping sounds of mechanical music.

There, in the den, appreciating these weapons, my uncle and dad rarely talked of actually firing them, or, for that matter, of hunting, crime, or personal protection. Even before Pearl Harbor, as a new engineering graduate himself, my dad had worked at the Philadelphia Navy Yard, on the great shipboard cannons of battleships meant to take on the Nazis and the Japanese. George, I think, was an ordinary G.I. But I never heard either of them talk of weapons fired in anger.

Sometimes during these years, my dad took me to a rifle range located, improbably enough, in downtown Manhattan's financial district. It was called the Manhattan School of Firearms and was located a couple of levels underground in a building on Murray Street near where the doomed Twin Towers would go up a few years later. You'd install yourself in one of the row of stalls, take up your rifle, using its leather sling and sometimes a special jacket and leather glove to steady it, line up front and rear sights on the bull's-eye and squeeze off your shot. When you'd taken your last shot, the flick of a switch summoned the target on its carrier back to you, so you could see how you'd done.

The rifles we used on this 50-foot range were twenty-twos, which made the barest kick or pop. This was marksmanship in miniature. The whole "black" of the target, with its higher-scoring inner rings, was not much more than an inch across, the bulls-eye itself only about an eighth of an inch in diameter. Each shot registered as a raggedy round tear in the paper, with a tinge of gray from the lead. Accuracy was an exercise in breathing; between the comparatively raucous quiverings of the human breath, you had to find just the right time to imperceptibly increase trigger pressure enough for the rifle to fire. It was a world of bloodless finesse, redolent with the sweet smell of gunpowder, nothing in the least scary about it, precise, technical, and fun.

When I was 11, I joined the Boy Scouts, a troop near our house that met in a nearby synagogue basement. It took me most of the next two years to climb out of the lowest rank, Tenderfoot; when it came to woodcraft and kindred skills, I lacked the ambition to advance. But I did become active in the Brooklyn Boy

Scout Marksmanship Program. On Saturdays, Dad would drive me to the farthest reaches of Brooklyn, facing Staten Island, since gobbled up by the approaches to the Verrazano-Narrows Bridge. There I earned colorful embroidered badges testifying to my progress through the sharpshooter ranks. Then, at Stuyvesant, I was on the rifle team. You could see me on the subway, openly carrying a long, cushioned vinyl bag, rifle within, to high school matches.

So during my early teen years, I did my school work, read Sinclair Lewis, John Dos Passos, and Ayn Rand, and inhabited the edge of the manly world of guns and ammo. I never shot anything but a target. I never killed anything. I never saw anybody or any animal shot—except for me, actually, when one Election Day, when I was 12 and playing in the basement, I shot myself in the hand with an air rifle; my poor parents, just back from voting, had to haul me off to a doctor to extract the lead pellet from my bloody hand.

My dad's mouthy friend Sid did exhibit some of the cruder gun-toting stereotypes; right there in our living room, he'd haul out his long-barreled .357 Magnum revolver and, all bluster, show it off. But otherwise, gun talk could be pretty tame, usually less macho than technical, especially among the fraternity of "reloaders," who experimented with non-standard bullets and powder loads. Sometimes my dad and Uncle George would take me to gun shows, with their displays of beautiful old muskets or other rare and wonderful specimens. At 14, I *had* to touch them, my father forever warning me to keep my hands clasped behind my back. After sophomore year of college, my interest in weaponry got me a job. After a first working summer at $1.35 an hour as an office temp in Manhattan, my job the following summer took me to Watervliet Arsenal, across the Hudson River from Rensselaer. This government arsenal didn't make rifles but rather, since the War of 1812, cannon—enormous things, made on gargantuan lathes and milling machines, in great cavernous halls, objects as big as you can imagine, and bigger than that, for tanks and artillery. Here was a world of machined and polished steel, parts made not just to strict dimension, but to specified "surface finish," defined by numbers corresponding to their almost invisible molecular ridges and irregularities: Needlessly smooth was just as bad as too rough, because it was expensive to get them that way.

I worked for Roy, who wrote quality control manuals, which specified how a cannon's breech-block, say, was to be measured, with which gauges, in what order; they had pages of black and white photographs that conveyed nothing whatever of the sheer mechanical artistry of the individual parts. The great, room-sized barrels of these cannon really did look menacing; but other cannon parts, like many in weaponry, could look like shining geometries of modern sculpture, glimmering in the half-light of the factory floor.

The following summer, I landed a job at Winchester, the maker of the famous Winchester 94 lever-action rifle, in New Haven, Connecticut. I made 110 bucks a week, double what I could have made, even full-time, at McDonalds. In those declining days of American manufacturing, Winchester occupied an industrial landscape almost unchanged since the 19th century. Think of a gentrified post-industrial city neighborhood today, like Baltimore's Fells Point or Toronto's Distillery District, the doors of old buildings opening onto restaurants and handicraft shops. But in the summer of 1965, "gentrification" was not even a word, and New Haven's brick factory buildings were still workshops, the streets and sidewalks around them crowded with workmen, not tourists. In one building, wooden stocks were automatically cut to size and shape. In another, a turret lathe, all mechanical choreography, took swipes at parts, steel chips curling up around the tool bits, cutting fluid raining down to keep them cool, all set against the smell of burnt oil.

I was still just a college student, but far enough along by now that they could give me a real job. My project was a four-barreled shotgun, a weapon truly of its time. The civil rights movement had left black people bent on equality, justice, and simple fairness—and angry. The year before, Harlem had erupted in riot. Three months before, Malcolm X was assassinated. And LA's Watts neighborhood would go up in flames that summer. Riot was in the air. Whites panicked.

My short-barreled weapon, black and menacing, was supposed to intimidate would-be looters and rioters with its specter of fearsome firepower at the press of a finger. Or rather, at the squeeze of a hand: I was working on a squeeze grip to enable you to use the strength of your whole hand to bring each of the four firing pins in line with the hammer. This brutal, ugly weapon mirrored the toxic atmosphere of our office—which was gleefully, horrifically, shockingly racist. One co-worker, a southerner, expressed open delight at the prospect of black rioters shredded by shot spewing from those four barrels.

I don't think our scary-assed shotgun ever came to anything. But the following year, as graduation neared and I went looking for a job, my weapons pedigree—I'd even done a term paper, incomplete though it was, on internal ballistics—by now added up to something. After several "plant trips," paid junkets to interview with would-be employers, I landed a number of offers, among them one from the Ammo Lab. *Kismet*. The company got a young engineer who liked guns. I got launched on my professional trajectory, with a good job that promised to be interesting, and was.

5

Back at Rensselaer, when I felt bored or frustrated studying for an exam, I'd sometimes rummage through the library stacks, dipping into books whose subjects were as far removed from differential equations or kinematics as I could find; think of it as aimless web-browsing before the internet. And now, at the Ammo Lab, I did it, too. My employer was dwarfed by the really big arms makers. But it was big enough to have its own technical library, its little warren of shelves with books enough to distract me for a while. I'd sometimes feel guilty, because I knew that whatever I stumbled on was little apt to help me in the work I did at my desk or drafting table. Still, when I needed to get away, that's where I went.

At the time, I didn't note the title of the book I discovered one day early in 1967. But very likely it's the one I tracked down recently during a Google search, a 1962 book published by the U.S. Army Surgeon General's office. Its subject was wound ballistics, a study of the effects of German weaponry on American air crews over Europe during World War II. There was more to it than that but that's the part I remember.

Books and documentaries cast the air war over Germany as a sweeping, heroic story of massed formations of American B-17 and B-24 bombers and their British counterparts, hundreds of them at a time, lined up over German factories and cities, out to destroy the Nazi evil. Joseph Heller, a veteran of 60 bombing runs over Italy, based his novel *Catch-22* on them. The war work of English physicist Freeman Dyson, before he turned writer, included compiling statistics on the chances of survival for British bomber crews. There was glory in the flights of those bombers, engulfed by black puffs of anti-aircraft fire, attacked by Messerchmitts and Focke-Wulfs, going down over Germany or limping home to fly another day.

I believe this story is true as far as it goes. But in the book I found that day in the library, it was told in a different way, by a different teller, for a different purpose. Opening the book to a random page, I saw corpses of every description. One with a neat hole the size of a dinner plate in the dead man's chest, as if a giant cookie cutter had punched through it. Or a naked shoulder, unmarked, the torso to which it should have been connected gone, the boundary of the wound black with blood. A chin, and only a chin—all that was left of a head, perfectly preserved. I saw images of men who hours before had been flying over Ploesti or Schweinfurt reduced to hamburger. I turned the pages and gagged. I'd absorb the sight of a headless cadaver, look away, but always come back, lured by the horrific, pornographic attraction of it. I looked until I could look no more. Briefly I'd pause on a page of verbal description, a data summary or chart, but mostly I'd flip past them, impatient to bring the next human monstrosity beneath my gaze.

"Multiple mutilating wounds," a caption might record, as if caption were needed. Or "partial decapitation." I'd linger at a nose shot off, the rest of the face intact; at a torso intact save for a silver dollar-sized hole through the heart, then look away once more. Here, under the heading of "wound ballistics," was what exploding anti-aircraft shells and machine gun fire did to human beings, their bodies the witness plates of war.

The war in Vietnam, if you date it to the Tonkin Gulf Resolution of August 1964 when American forces were first committed, had been going on for two years by now. I little remember how I felt about it when I started at the Ammo Lab, but I don't think I thought about it much; it was going on far away, against an Asian people who were supposed to be our enemy. When, soon after I started, my boss, Jay Kleiner, a genial and intelligent man in his thirties, explained to me the purpose of our 20mm APDS ammunition, he didn't mention the Viet Cong or the North Vietnamese but the Soviets, and their tanks, and how we needed to be able to destroy them. Vietnam's fate was caught up in America's worldwide struggle against Communism. This was the prevalent assumption of the day.

But the photos in the wound ballistics book eclipsed assumption and abstraction. I went back to look at them again and again, re-experiencing the gore, trolling through them, my eyes big with wonder and disgust. I was mortified by my own fascination. The images lodged there, permanently, at the edge of consciousness, sometimes rearing up, impossible to ignore. I could not unsee them.

Of course, I *did* nothing, so the outward effect of those pictures on my life was precisely zero. They did not abruptly turn me against the war. I did not start showing up at anti-war demonstrations. I went back to work. And yet, I had begun to discern some dim connection between the work I did for a living, the mangled witness plates at the range, the shredded corpses in the book, the mounting casualty lists from Vietnam, and the scenes of death and devastation on the evening news.

The following excerpt is from book 3 of the *Iliad*:

Suddenly Paris hurled—his spear's long shadow flew and the shaft hit Menelaus' round shield, full center—not pounding through, the brazen point bent back in the tough armor.

The spear, Homer tells us, *doesn't* get through. Likewise in book 7, when a spear strikes Ajax's shield: "Through six hides it tore but the seventh stopped the relentless brazen point."

All through history, men have wielded swords, arrows, and lances against shields and body armor. They have made arrowheads from flakes of stone, quartz, or obsidian, notched and scraped into their familiar forms; experts today can tie them by design and material to this historical epoch, that tribe or battle. With each improvement, with each more "relentless brazen point," the tribal hunter came home with more game, the warrior was left more able to defeat his enemy and live to fight another day. What we did at the Ammo Lab, then, stood in this ancient tradition.

I wasn't thinking much about Homer in those days. But the same avid, even technical interest Homer evokes in, say, the shield Hephaestus makes for Achilles in Book 18 is not so far from what motivated us at the Ammo Lab. Spurring us to improve our product were our ammo's failings—that it didn't yet work as well as it might. Sometimes, the flechette failed to reach its proper velocity, the sabots that were supposed to grip it within the barrel sometimes failing to do so; we tried sandblasting the flechette surface to give the sabots a better hold. Often, the flechettes weren't as accurate as a conventional round, wobbling in flight. And we worried that clouds of discarded sabots might be sucked into the jet engines of our own planes, destroying them, the way flocks of birds occasionally threaten commercial airliners; we never resolved that one.

Among my colleagues, only one of them did anything like the work I'd thought, back in college, constituted real engineering work. His name was Dan Stavak and he was the theorist of our office, the analyst, the one who, back at school, would have been most at home among symbols, Greek letters, and mathematical proofs. If you were trying to find out whether a part would break or a flechette would wobble in flight, you'd go around to Stavak's desk, which was around the corner from where we rank-and-file engineers and draftsmen worked, and describe the problem. A few days later he'd hand you a stress analysis or other mathematics-riddled treatment, all in pencil, that began to make sense of things.

But Stavak was the exception. The others I worked with arranged for test firings, prepared drawings, recorded data, put in part modifications, wrote progress reports—in short, at one or two removes from the analytical work we'd struggled with in school. But they—that is, we—were the arms industry, too. We all kept it going. The Ammo Lab was no gargantuan enterprise, but it was big enough to have secretaries and security guards, technical writers and administrators. There were meetings to hold, paper to order, new employees to sign up, reports to get out.

We had a photographer, too, whose job was to take pictures of test rigs, charts and new design features for progress reports and other documents. This was Charlie Cavallaro, who wasn't much older than I, if he was older at all, yet had somehow acquired enough experience to preside over a fiefdom of his own. He was dark-haired and full-lipped, with a pleasantly soft New Jersey accent, bubbly in his enthusiasms. I liked him and often found a reason to visit his studio.

His was a world apart. At the machine shop and the firing range, real things were made, tested, blown apart. Here, they were propped up for a picture, just so, under the right lighting, this or that feature in or out of focus. Charlie's studio was one of bright lights, reflectors, and bulky view cameras, all knobs and bellows, which, when mounted on tripods, could be brought up as near as you liked to some minute detail or pulled back for a group portrait. There was a *thinginess* to Charlie's domain I liked. I'd never been the iconic engineer, forever building and taking apart. But I did like mechanical things *as* things, tactilely and aesthetically—the suspension cables on the great New York bridges, the heavy nickel anodes in my father's shop. It was one reason I liked guns, for their steely heft.

Now, alongside Charlie, I got the photography bug. I bought a new camera. Not the usual 35mm with the little bitty negative ubiquitous before the digital revolution, but a clunky twin-lens reflex, a Japanese copy of the famous Rolleiflex, with a big square negative whose image you could blow up in the dark room with scant loss of detail. Unusually, for someone as young as I, it wasn't action and movement, or Henri Cartier-Bresson's famous "decisive moment," that attracted me, but the theatrically lit portraits of an Edward Steichen or Yousuf Karsh, or the formal, color-saturated still-lifes of Marie Cosindas.

In the end, photography for me proved simply a hobby; it could as easily have been gardening, gun collecting, or antique restoration. I enjoyed it and began to get good at it. I learned, took classes, joined a club, was in and out of camera shops. And over the next few years, it was among cameras and film, dark rooms and fixing baths, lights and lenses that you'd be most apt to find me. If photography were a person, it would be something like Zelig for me, the fictional character in the Woody Allen film who always seemed to show up at meaningful moments. Later, I'd wonder if maybe it served as a step away from engineering, a way out, a link to the arts and humanities that helped draw me out of my old life—before writing drew me away more urgently.

It's a nice idea, and it might have seemed that way from the outside. But I don't think it's true. Certainly, it did nothing to extract me from the arms industry.

Sometime early in 1967, when I'd been on the job for less than a year, a new wind blew through the

Ammo Lab. For reasons never clear to me, several of the company's best engineers left, all of them bound for a much smaller company on the other side of town named Miller Research Corporation. Miller was suddenly the place to be. Dave left to go there. So did Ed. Even my photographer friend, Charlie, left. And me? Well, I left, too. Not yet 21, I joined the parade in April 1967.

Miller was a much smaller version of my former employer, with only about 100 people, occupying a one-story building in a cheerless area south of downtown Baltimore. But its ranks had almost doubled in the previous two years and it was supposed to be technologically innovative. Its work was war-related almost entirely, only on a smaller scale; I'm tempted to say on a more "human scale," but the irony is just too chilling. None of the projects I knew of at first-hand were so death-dealing as our 20mm APDS ammo, though that didn't figure in my move. One was a grapnel fired from a standard grenade launcher to help troops ford streams and climb hills. Another was a position marker. A third was an improved machete. All served, or were inspired by, the war in Vietnam. Most were under contract with the US Army Limited War Laboratory, rooted in America's new military realities: The set-piece battles of World War II were history. Vietnam was all hidden enemies and insidious jungle fighting.

I was assigned to work on something called

Lift-a-Rig, which was intended to salvage duds—bombs dropped in the jungle that failed to go off. This improbable contraption consisted of a pulley traversing a light-weight beam erected on tripods; each component needed to be light enough for a soldier to carry into the jungle. Assembled at the site, the bomb could then be hoisted from its jungle bed and safely disarmed. One time we set up a prototype that actually hauled up a half-ton welding machine, our stand-in for a bomb. But if Lift-a-Rig ever saw service in Vietnam, I never heard about it.

On the surface, Miller was just more skinny ties and drafting tables. But a certain madcap energy ran through it, too, all of us given rein to come up with new gizmos, try them, land a contract, and get them built. At one point we flirted with the idea of a miniature hot-air balloon for use in jungle signaling—something like the colorful paper lanterns set aloft on Caribbean wedding days. It was a charming idea, and I did some simple thermodynamic calculations to see how much it could lift. Of course it, like everything else we did at Miller, served the war.

I was put on one job where even the name of the contractor was secret, though the sheer cloak-and-dagger of it made it hard not to think of the CIA: It was a chemical timer designed to fire a bomb at some set time in the future, once our guys, presumably, were out of the way. Today, it would be the work of fifty cents' worth of electronic circuitry. But back then, our Rube Goldberg thing was built around a chemical bath designed to eat through a thin cable at a set rate; 24 hours later, say, the cable would break, releasing a spring-driven firing pin to set off the bomb. One weekend, I brought it home to test, setting it to fire a small explosive primer. I forgot about it, only to have the weekend's repose with my girlfriend shattered when, right on schedule, the thing went off.

That summer, I got a more substantial scare: I'd been reclassified 1-A, meaning I could be called up for military service at any time. It seems that neither I nor my new employer had notified my draft board that I had a new defense job. But soon the company president himself wrote them, noting that Miller was "100% engaged in classified Government contract work in the fields of ordnance, pyrotechnics and various military weapons systems"; that I was doing Department of Defense R & D; that I held a Secret clearance; and that my loss to the company "would entail a considerable replacement problem" to find someone with my abilities. This last was bunk, and it isn't mistaken modesty to say so; I might in time have become a good engineer, but I certainly wasn't then, barely out of school. Still, my 2-A occupational deferment was reinstated.

It was around this time that Charlie, my photographer friend, returned from his trip to a jungle testing site someplace far away. I wasn't supposed to know just where, or just what they'd been testing. But I deduced it was one of those creepy projects the Limited War Laboratory loved—an anti-personnel weapon for use in the first frightening moments of a jungle ambush, giving our soldiers a few precious seconds to regroup. If I've got it right, it shot out streams of burning magnesium, known to cling to flesh as it burned. They tried it out on pigs—this much, at least, Charlie told me—and it worked fine. He reported this with no horror, no taint of moral judgment, just big-eyed wonder at the blood and death and gore he'd seen and photographed.

During 1967, my views of the war, like those of so many other Americans, began to change. In March, Greta wrote me from her Peace Corps post. "Sounds like you've got quite a good fight going on inside your head. May the best head win!" Had I been troubled by the war even before the move to Miller?

In May, on a trip to New York, I saw the play *MacBird* at the Village Gate. This was Barbara Garson's brilliantly caustic reimagining of Shakespeare's *Macbeth*, with MacBird—President Lyndon Johnson, of course, whose wife was known as Lady Bird—presiding over the war, determined to mercilessly crush the Asian enemy: "MacBird's gone mad, a killer turned berserk/Each morn new widows' wails, new orphan cries/Howl up to heaven." The whole play—hilarious, incisive, cruel—reeked of the madness of war. Certainly of *this* war.

As hellish videos from Vietnam spun across the evening news, millions of young Americans interrogated their own beliefs. In the war, they saw either stupidity, cruelty, and immorality, or a last stand against international communism. They read, questioned, and doubted. They weighed their own notions of bravery and patriotism. I was among them. I concluded I was no pacifist. "Only the force of allied arms," my father said, had stopped the Nazis; I couldn't be against all war, for all time. But *this* war, it seemed to me by now, was senseless and sick. The contradictions were just too much to bear. How many times had I squirmed to Bob Dylan's scathing "Masters of War"?

Come you masters of war
You that build all the guns
You that build the death planes
You that build all the bombs

"My, you're rather bitter these days!" Greta replied to one of my letters. She went on to tell of the good, peaceful work she was doing in Guatemala, of women's and girls' sewing classes, village gardens, first-aid treatments, a new library. She had taught one villager to do woodcuts; his design adorned her letter's translucent orange pages. She'd been able to travel a bit, had seen a volcano up close, visited Mayan ruins. True, there were "guerillas all over the country, but somehow we don't feel any threat or panic about it. Guys get knocked off every day, government officials are threatened. Bombs are thrown at buildings, but Peace Corps goes on with its idealistic head in the clouds, with only visions of peace before its eyes!

"So, my friend in brown suede," she finished up, "what goes with you now that fall is on the scene again? (Sure miss that weather!) Change jobs again? What's happening with 'Weapons for Peace'?" I don't know now and maybe didn't know then, either. I folded up her letter, slipped it back into its envelope, and went back to work on my chemical timer.

That was late September. Less than a month later, on the morning of October 21, I was issued a little blue card that counted as my bus ticket, marked "FALL MOBILIZATION TO CONFRONT THE WARMAKERS." I was one of the warmakers myself, but I was on my way to Washington to protest the war.

The March on the Pentagon was the first big nationally scaled anti-war rally, with over one hundred thousand protesters. Boarding the bus, we'd been issued the day's timetable: Rally at the Lincoln Memorial at 11:30, march across the Potomac bridge to the Pentagon beginning at 1:30, rally at the Pentagon at 3:30. At 4 pm: "Direct Action: peaceful sit-in for those who wish to participate."

At the Lincoln Memorial, I didn't scream or shout or hoot, just listened to the songs and speeches; I don't remember them now. But later, once we'd crossed the Potomac and reached the steps of the Pentagon, where federal troops would arrest 600 demonstrators, this I well recall: The ranks of troops, hundreds or thousands of them, helmeted, armed with rifles, standing straight and tall, all impressively identical, immobile, impassive. And us—and for the first time for me, it *was* us!—crowded, shifting masses of us, in jeans, sloppy and ragtag. Except that the way I learned to see that day, there were better, sweeter adjectives to use—easy, loose, flexible, and free. Before the march, there'd been some charming, zany talk about how we would "levitate" the Pentagon, set it loose from its foundations, have it just float away and so end the war. And looking at us, in all our shining energy, maybe we could!

Later, pictures taken that day showed demonstrators proffering flowers to unflinching soldiers. I'd swear I saw it in front of me, but maybe the ubiquity of the image has corrupted my memory. What I know for sure, though, was the stark split between the line of soldiers and our irregular protesting tides. Two ways of life. Not just of war and peace, violence and love, rigid authority vs. questioning and protest. But two distinct, deep-lying visions. There, on the steps of the Pentagon, I looked at the soldiers and knew, *I don't want to be like them.* I saw us and knew I belonged where I was, with people like us, people like me.

The March on the Pentagon took place on a

Saturday. The following Monday, my first day back at work, or maybe it was a day or two later, I quit my job. I went in to talk with Carl, my boss, a good man. There, in his corner office, I sat across from him and explained I could no longer do the work I'd been doing. I couldn't do war work anymore. Yet I didn't *quite* quit all at once. Perhaps there was a more convenient way out of my predicament? I'd heard talk of Miller moving in new directions, I told Carl, of the same creative approaches we brought to military work applied to a different, entirely benign field—mail handling. The U.S. Post Office, it was said, desperately needed new technology to lower its costs. I wanted to stay at Miller, I told Carl. I liked the company. I liked my colleagues. It's just that I couldn't do war work any longer. Could I be transferred to this new project?

No, Carl wearily explained, there was no new project. The Post Office work was still just talk. If Miller was going in that direction, it wouldn't be right away, or even soon, or maybe ever. Just now there was nothing.

So I gave notice.

6

In 1967, being a jobless 21-year-old male meant being vulnerable to the draft, and probably going to war—the very war I'd served in the job I'd just quit. Back in August, while briefly 1-A, I'd actually been called for my pre-induction physical; I'd gone down to Fort Meade, been measured, probed, and pricked, had my blood drawn, and been pronounced, in the words of the official notice, "fully acceptable for induction into the armed forces."

But then, once Miller had appealed on my behalf, my 2-A had come through.

Now, I'd be 1-A all over again.

"Are you a conscientious objector [CO] to war?" That's what one of the many fliers and broadsides I collected during this period asked. This one came from a Philadelphia-based group of COs. I reviewed the definitions, read the fine print, but saw no way to claim I was a conscientious objector. The Philadelphia group was advising, "*Do not assume you do not qualify.*" Even if you were an atheist. Some draft boards were surprisingly liberal in their interpretations. Still, even by the loosest standards, I didn't see how I could qualify—not by religious training, personal belief, or any other way. The Vietnam war was monstrously wrong, and I'd do nothing to further it. But, in principle—*"...Only the force of Allied arms..."*—I saw a place for war.

I saw but one option—Canada, to which some Americans were already emigrating. There, up north, across that long undefended frontier, lay big, open-hearted Canada, presided over by its telegenic premier, Pierre Trudeau, opening its doors, opening its arms. By some counts, 50,000 Americans would ultimately emigrate, live out the war years there, and often the rest of their lives. In the weeks after I left Miller, it seemed not just possible, not just likely, but almost certain that I would be among them.

There were established ways to get to Canada and plenty of advice on how to do it. The Southern Student Organizing Committee of Nashville issued "Emigration to Canada: Legal Notes for Draft-Age Men." The Committee to Aid American War Objectors, out of Vancouver, detailed what you had to do beforehand and what you might expect in Canada on arrival.

At the downtown Baltimore library, I found a booklet, *Working and Living Conditions in Canada,* larded with facts and figures and filled with pretty views of diverse Canadian settings; a power station going up in Saskatchewan; Canadians on vacation at a provincial park in Manitoba or sitting around picnic tables along Lake Ontario. Altogether it lent reassuring wholesomeness to what had by now begun to feel like my new country. "Newcomers to Canada" should expect conditions different from their home country "and should not be disappointed if they do not immediately obtain the kind of work in which they are most interested." That could sound like a warning. But by now, while the Stars and Stripes conjured up GIs destroying Vietnamese villages in order to "save" them, Canada's Maple Leaf represented decency and welcome. From almost the beginning, it was plain to me that Canada meant Montreal. I had relatives there— my mother's first cousin and her husband. I still had my *Dollar-Wise Guide* to the city, from a recent visit to the world's fair, Expo 67. I'd enjoyed the city's Gallic flavoring and silent rubber-tired subway. I had some high school French under my belt. I resolved to go, leave America, soon, and delivered the news to my parents.

My father called and said he wanted to come down to Baltimore to talk to me. In August, the family had moved from the Brooklyn house in which I'd grown up, and in which my grandparents still lived, to a split-level in Bergen County, New Jersey, a place probably twice the size of the Brooklyn apartment, with a two-car garage and plenty of lawn.

For my parents, it must have been a treat to finally make the big move to the suburbs that many of their friends had already made. They were by now in their mid-forties. Dad was starting to look a little jowly. He still ran the original Williamsburg, Brooklyn, plating shop, but now had a second one in Jersey; he had become, he joked, "a business typhoon." And now, a few weeks after the Pentagon protest, he was in Baltimore, in the apartment I shared with my girl-friend, Bev, his chair backed up against the wall, silent at first, marshaling his thoughts, preparing one of his familiar preambles.

For anything important he had to say, my father never just blurted it out. Rather, he'd carefully frame it, enmesh it in context, place his real point in oppo-sition or contrast to its opposite. Maybe it was a leftover of studying Talmud as a boy. Or a bent for what rhetoricians called dialectics, finding new truth in opposing half-truths. In any case, this was the way his mind worked. I knew it was coming, I waited for it patiently, and sure enough there it was:

Yes, he said, he could well understand my feel-ings about the war. (Our family did not exactly boast a warrior tradition.) And he could understand the urgency I felt about acting quickly; the wheels of The Draft were spinning fast, processing soldiers by the thousands for the maw of Vietnam. Quitting Miller had no doubt already triggered the bureaucratic steps that would make me 1-A and, soon enough, cannon fodder. So yes, my father said, if I felt the way I did about the war and going to Canada, then certainly, by all means, I should go.

I should go, he went on, but—and here it was, the *turn*, the interrupted cadence, the surprise kicker that was so much part of his style—not quite yet. Very soon, certainly, but not immediately.

For how, he asked, could I be sure I wouldn't find a job that, while untainted by war work and thoroughly benign, might nonetheless offer an occupational deferment? Indeed, he'd come down with a Selective Service System brochure in hand, "Information for Employers," that set out the requirements for occupational deferments, its key provisions underlined. Crucial was "the function of your organization as it pertains to the national health, safety, or interest," and how the employee contributed to it through a "critical skill" or "essential activity." No mention of defense work.

True, a deferment was no foregone conclusion if you weren't making guns or fighter jets. But it *was* possible; the rules didn't say you had to work for the war, so long as you contributed to the nation's welfare. So, concluded my father, I should go to Montreal if it came to that. But first, over the next month or so, might I not try to find just such a job, one that would leave me with a clean conscience, free of the war, free of the draft, and still in America?

My dad's speech, I suppose, might be seen as rank parental meddling. Here he was, uninvited, stepping in to his grown son's life, advising him what to do. The son, we might guess, would rebel, reflexively saying, "No, I'll do it my way." But I didn't. I bought into his thinking: *If you want to go, go. But hold off just now.* And that's what I agreed to do.

My dad returned to New York, and I went looking for this needle-in-a-haystack dream job. Actually, I wasn't even that stressed about it. I would find such a job or I was off to Montreal; either would be OK. Jobs were plentiful just then, the unemployment rate below 4 per cent. Over the next month, my daybook filled with penciled-in calls and appointments with old-line American companies like Koppers, Western Electric, and Ward-Turner. Through Mike, a wire-service reporter friend, I met with an editor he knew; maybe some entry- level job in journalism? Nothing worked out.

But then one morning toward the end of December, two months after the Pentagon demonstration, I took a bus out to Joppa Road, in the suburbs, for an interview at Bendix, a maker of car radios. That led to a second interview, at a job fair in downtown Baltimore, where I was to meet Dave Vincent from the company's Automotive Electronics Division. Dave was a tall, craggy, athletic looking man, a Navy veteran, around 40. We met. We clicked. He told me I had the job, and that he was pretty sure he could get me a draft deferment.

I started at Bendix the Tuesday after New Year's Day.

⌣

For two decades, my new employer had been known as Bendix Radio, and thousands of AM and FM car radios still poured off its assembly lines at its big Towson factory. Women, sitting close-packed together as radio carcasses passed slowly in front of them, inserted and soldered resistors, transistors, and capacitors. The line bubbled over with the smell of molten solder and burning flux, the radios filling up, ever more crowded with components, as they inched along the line.

But now it was 1969, and electronics in automobiles was not just radios. It was a time when computers still occupied whole rooms, before microprocessors did anything, much less everything; there was no such thing as a personal computer. But things were changing. Bendix Radio was now Bendix Automotive Electronics, which was taking baby steps toward self-driving cars and a new electronics-run world.

We had two main products. One was an automatic temperature control system, which opened valves, shut baffles, and changed fan speeds to flood the passenger compartment with cooled or heated air. This was already a going business and we supplied them by the tens of thousands to Ford and Chrysler. The other product, a new one, scarcely off the drawing boards, was an automatic speed control: Click a switch to set the desired speed and, notwithstanding hills or wavering attention, you'd keep to that speed until you tapped the brake pedal—particularly useful on long drives on the open road. That was the party line, anyway; I thought it useless frippery. In any case, we had developed its components—a speed sensor, a throttle actuator, an electronics pack—and had set up a factory on Quad Avenue, in an industrial suburb east of the city, to make them. I was among a group of engineers whose job was to shepherd it into production.

The speed control needed to be made for twenty-five dollars apiece; that's what Ford was paying if we could make them to spec, which mostly we couldn't. "Tolerance accumulation" was one reason: An assembly of one part made to tolerance, a second made to tolerance, and a third made to tolerance, once you put them all together, sometimes didn't work at all, or even fit together. You'd get rubbing and scraping, or a housing that had to be hammered shut, or a valve that wouldn't open at all, or who knows what other costly, maybe dangerous mechanical glitch.

My older, more jaded colleagues would sit at their desks, bitching, blaming the women on the line at Quad for anything that didn't work. But so far as I could see, the problems lay in the original design, were virtually built in to it. I identified some of them and, a month into the job, got a note from Dave's boss that I was doing well and should keep it up.

The following month, it was time to test Dave's assurance that he could get me an occupational deferment. The personnel department had sent my draft board what was probably a boilerplate letter testifying to my worth. It was not enough. I was summoned to New York to defend myself in person. My dad drove me to an office in downtown Brooklyn, left me to step into a room, alone, with a big table around which sat my inquisitors.

But Dave Vincent had come through with a letter to the board explaining just why my work was so important to Bendix and the nation. "With the increased consumer and Federal Government emphasis on safety and quality of automotive products," he wrote—Ralph Nader's indictment of the auto industry, *Unsafe at Any Speed,* had been a recent best-seller—"key men like Mr. Kanigel are needed." As for the automatic temperature control, absent the "searching investigation" he imagined me making of "the variables which go into this product's market demand and satisfaction" (I didn't know what that meant either) Bendix would fall fatally behind its competitors.

Then Dave raised the rhetorical pitch one note higher. It wasn't just Bendix profits, or driver safety and comfort, that were at stake: The country's well-being depended on the automotive industry. "In the event of total mobilization for war or increased requirements for mass-produced weapons of defense," he wrote, Bendix represented a "recognized resource in America's arsenal." And I, young Mr. Kanigel, was crucial to this overarching defense need: I wasn't doing war work, but I *could*.

At the draft board in Brooklyn, I was asked questions. I answered them. After it was over, my dad picked me up. I returned to Baltimore, to wait.

Soon enough, the verdict was rendered: I got the deferment. I didn't have to disrupt my life one iota. I could go back to my girlfriend, my cameras, and my darkroom, and to a job with every prospect of advancement, all without taint to my conscience.

———

Bendix was a pretty good gig, really. Even within this big corporation, I enjoyed autonomy. I often stayed late at my desk and drawing board, and so felt comfortable wandering in late the next morning. Come lunchtime, on a good day, I'd camp out on the outdoor stairway behind the office and bask in the sun with my bag lunch and a book. Among my colleagues at Bendix, my boss Dave stood out from the others in his liberal and thoughtful way; you could *talk* to him about things.

Standing out, too, if in quite another way, was puffy, red-cheeked Harlan, who giggled his way through each day, managing to work as little as possible; but at least he had a recognizable personality, which most of my colleagues lacked. Many were older versions of the boys and young men with whom I'd gone to college, except that instead of preparing for jobs in industry, they *had* jobs in industry, going home at five to their wives and children.

Meanwhile, in photography I had a hobby I liked. I was taking portraits—stiff, formal portraits, to be sure, but I enjoyed paying careful heed to the play of light on my subject's face and fidgeting with the final print. I'd converted a closet into a tiny, bare-bones dark room, which perfumed the apartment with the smell of chemicals. Later I rented a basement across Calvert Street, for $20 a month, and made it into a more spacious dark room, together with an area large enough to set up lights for studio portraits; my inspiration was Yousuf Karsh, who made the famous picture of a scowling Winston Churchill. As my interest and experience grew, my portfolio thickened, and I flirted with starting up a side business. I had some cards made up. They read:

From the suede left over from Greta's jacket, Bev sewed me up a little case in which to hold them.

Bev was my new fiancée.

7

Soon after I'd arrived in Baltimore, almost in parallel with my romantic adventures downtown, Sandor and Penny had taken to lining up dates for me. Sandor, who I'd met in the fencing club in college, was a refugee from the Hungarian Revolution who'd come here with his family after 1956, adapted brilliantly to his new country, and excelled as a chemical engineer. When I first landed in Baltimore, he was the only person I knew. Voluble, instinctively upbeat, he and his future wife Penny were soon fixing me up with young Baltimore women of their acquaintance.

One of them was Karen, who I picked up at her parents' big house in the suburbs and drove off with, probably to a movie and dinner. I don't remember much about the evening except that she was pretty, poised, and unreachable. We had zero chemistry. When I dropped her off at her home later, I drove off feeling distanced and bad. Had Sandor asked, I might have said I'd had a nice time. But I don't think I knew what a nice time was, or meant, or could mean. I didn't know much about my heart or anyone else's.

Bev Shorr was another friend of Sandor's, a junior high school classmate of Penny's who made for a far more consequential story. She was still in school, an undergraduate psychology major at Goucher College, which occupied a spacious green campus just north of the city. She was beautiful, smart, with a girlish sweetness, a trim figure, and long brown hair she wore straight or up in a bun. Soon we were seeing each other regularly. One day we spent the day around Mt. Vernon Place, snapping pictures, Bev posed against some of the classic bronze sculptures adorning the square, her hair this time in fetching little pigtails.

She lived in Mt. Washington in the leafy outskirts of the city, with her father, an engineer, her over-anxious mother, and her younger brother, just then busily into his flute but destined for a career as a physician. I admired her father, who worked for the federal government and who, in best *Father Knows Best*-style, really did seem to know best.

Nice house. Nice family. Nice girl.

At one point, Bev and I talked about going up to Montreal to see Expo 67, the world's fair, but she worried her parents might object. We were in my little apartment at the time, the one I'd taken over from Edwin and Merrily. It was dark, I held her close, and reassured her that we needn't defer to her parents, that she could decide for herself. Why worry about what they might say? I remember feeling masculine and wise in offering this brilliant advice, with all the strength and certainty a man, I guessed, was sup-posed to possess, but with scant concern for how she would manage with her mother and father, or how she might feel about defying them.

Sometime later, my lease was up, and I found a place two doors up the street, again in the basement, but with a big window that opened up on a sunken backyard and brought in plenty of natural light. It was a lot nicer than the cockroach-ridden mess Heidler's apartment had become, for all my fickle attentions. Bev and I moved in together. Out of a sheet of plywood, a few 2 x 4s, and a slab of thick foam rubber, I made us a bed. Bev, expert seamstress, fashioned a dramatic red and black cotton covering for it. From linked cardboard-backed posters—Milton Glaser's Bob Dylan, white-suited Bogey in *Casablanca*—we made a screen that transformed the undivided basement space into a living room, our sleeping alcove behind it.

In a picture I took of her after she moved in with me, Bev is sitting on the stool beside the counter that set off our small kitchen from the rest of the apartment, on the phone, hair streaming down, smoking. This was an ordinary snapshot. But by that time I fancied myself a serious photographer, and Bev would sometimes pose for me. I made one photo of her, nude but decorous, from the back, the floodlights dividing her figure into starkly black and white regions. I gave it what I thought sounded like an artistic title, submitted it to a camera club contest, and won something—a ribbon, I think.

I met some of Bev's Goucher friends. One was married to a social worker who ran a program for troubled youths. Another was married to Mike, the wire-service reporter, who introduced us to marijuana, poker evenings, and big-city journalism, and entertained us with choice tales of political corruption. Bev seemed to take to her downtown life with me.

Living together in our cozy place, we were doing well. My parents liked Bev—she was such a winning presence. As for Bev's parents, their early mistrust of me as suitor of their only daughter had dissipated. "Dear Bev," I wrote across a sheet of loose-leaf paper early one morning. "You are beautiful when you are asleep. You are beautiful always. Happy Thanksgiving. I love you."

In early summer of 1967—a year after I'd graduated from college, barely 21—I asked Bev to marry me. She said yes.

⌣‿‿‿⌣

As an engagement present, my parents gave us a table radio with a fine walnut cabinet. I still have it and still say of it, to myself or to friends who chance to notice it: *That's the radio my parents gave Bev and me for our engagement.* I say it as attestation. Evidence that I've led a regular life of ordinary incidents, events, and experiences, that mine is a life like any other, tied to those of others, that I'm not cut so differently from the Frankie Russos of the world.

Back when I first arrived in Baltimore after college, my new grown-up life had seemed unreal to me. I didn't recognize myself in it and was determined to hold onto every last bit of it that I could. One afternoon, an upstairs neighbor slipped a scribbled note through the mail slot: "There's an outdoor concert tonight at Patterson Park at 8:30. We both could use a little culture. Do you want to go?" The note was inconsequential, but I saved it.

That was the beginning. Whenever I went to a local amateur theater, Spotlighters, I saved the playbill. Likewise, the matte black matchbook from the Peabody Beer Stube, or a political flyer handed me on the street. At first, they fell into an aimless little pile. Then I started stowing them in a shoe box I kept in the dark hall behind my tiny kitchen—palpable proof to myself that I had a life. My collection grew. A magazine cartoon a colleague at work gave me. A wine label that had slipped off a bottle. I saved them all. In 2008, a Turkish writer, Orhan Pamuk, published a strange, obsessive novel, *The Museum of Innocence*, about his infatuation with a young woman and his resolve to collect every last physical remnant of her—the butt of a cigarette she smoked, the newspaper description of the TV program they watched together. I became a little like that. My shoebox supplied evidence of the things everyone else seemed to do and I didn't—but that now I did, too. I saved love letters. The price list for options on my car. A Christmas card from my boss at work. I was like a poor man, finally with a little money, turned greedy; I saved everything. A photograph of me at an Ammo Lab open house. The program from an anti-war documentary. A cryptic pencil drawing. The receipt for a sewing machine I bought Bev.

To me, these spoke of a familiar-enough life of ordinary human connection. And with Bev Shorr, I had every prospect of living it. We were, as I said, a good couple. We'd make a good family. We already had a coterie of friends together. I cared for her, enjoyed her company, delighted in her sense of humor, relished her physical loveliness, loved her in my boy-man way.

But Bev and I didn't marry. We never married. Something was wrong.

———

Some deep discontent? Some dark resentment? No, if anything was wrong, it was below the radar, or else hung over me like a fogbank, obscuring events, details, moments. Later, I would remember remarkably little of our life together, of what we did, what we talked about, how we lived, the dreams we must have had, the confidences we must have shared. What did this say about Bev? Nothing. About me? Too much: I was engaged to Bev, yet recalled so little? I was young. Did that give me leave to forget? Or for memories I did have to remain so stubbornly indistinct? Much later, this lapse embarrassed me. I reread letters Bev wrote me, after we split up, and these did help, especially with the littlest things. Opening a jar of instant coffee, Bev was reminded of how, when we were still together, I'd make a silly show of puncturing its taut paper membrane, deflowering it. Another time, she recalled the day my "national debt," the balance of my student debt, dipped below $3,000, and how happy she was for me.

We talked about the children we would have. We named our first son—Daniel. Reading through these letters, I felt her tenderness and warmth. Meanwhile, my old daybook from that year, Bev listed as "emergency contact," helped me reconstitute the outward shape of our lives together: A bar mitzvah in Long Island. A visit to my folks in their new house in New Jersey. We went over to the Weisses, Bev's friends, for dinner and to give them a babysitting break. And regularly to Mr. and Mrs. Shorr's for dinner. All the while I was the able, up-and-coming young engineer my education had prepared me to be. Outside of work, I kept at my photography, sat in on occasional poker games. On a Sunday in early June 1968, Bev graduated from Goucher; the next day she started a job at a downtown department store.

Review the evidence and there was nothing wrong. For us, things were good.

For the rest of America, though, things couldn't

have been worse. In Vietnam, soldiers died, ours, theirs; the names of 58,000 Americans would be inscribed on the black granite walls of the Vietnam War monument in Washington; three hundred thousand more wounded, 75,000 of them left disabled. And the dead weren't only soldiers, but civilians in the hundreds of thousands, their villages destroyed. The story wasn't yet known, but on March 16, 1968, in a place called My Lai, American soldiers raped, burned, and massacred their way through almost 500 unarmed villagers. Anti-war demonstrations grew more frequent, larger, angrier. Angry acts followed on angry words. The country *hurt*, hurt so bad.

On March 31, 1968, President Johnson, faced by insurrection within his own party, announced he would not run for reelection. He didn't mention the war; he didn't have to. Everyone saw that he'd been driven from office by the anti-war movement.

On April 4, Martin Luther King, Jr. was assassinated. The following weekend I went up to New York to take possession of an old car my grandfather had stopped driving and given to me; I'd unloaded my adorable but undependable sports car some months before, been carless since. When I returned, National Guardsmen in riot gear were patrolling the streets of Baltimore. Whole neighborhoods had burned to the ground, as they had in Chicago, Detroit, and Washington. The troops remained for a week. The city would never fully recover.

Then, at three in the morning on June 5, up late while Bev slept, listening to the radio for the much-awaited returns from the California presidential primary, I heard the news flash that Bobby Kennedy, just named winner in his hard-fought race with Gene McCarthy, had been shot. It happened in the back kitchen of a Los Angeles hotel. Bobby died early the next day.

These tumultuous events in the life of the country and the world all took place within an astonishingly brief period. All through it, Bev and I remained engaged, though we had not yet set a date for the wedding.

In July, two Ingmar Bergman films came to Baltimore. One was *The Seventh Seal*, the Swedish director's story of a medieval knight's confrontation with death. The other was *Wild Strawberries*, about an old man recollecting his life. Bev and I went to see it.

Isak Borg, a 78-year-old professor, is to be awarded an honorary degree at the university in Lund, capping a distinguished career in medicine, 50 years after graduation. *Wild Strawberries* recounts his day-long drive to Lund with Marianne, his daughter-in-law, who's estranged from her husband, Isak's son Evald. Along the way Isak talks with Marianne, picks up hitchhikers, drops in on his ancient mother, meets acquaintances from long ago, fitfully dreams and daydreams. The long, eventful drive throws old Isak back on his youth, to reflect on his relationships, to ruminate on his life and how he's lived it. In dream and memory, Isak is brought back to the summer house of his childhood and its wild strawberry patch. We see him in the long, ill-shapen overcoat of his current old age, shambling into the settings of his past, alone, apart, and confused. At Uncle Aron's birthday party, all full of hijinks and youthful energy, his sweetheart, Sara, pronounces him kind and earnest—but, oh, his brother Sigfrid is "so bold and exciting!" She ends up marrying Sigfrid, giving him six children. "You know so much," she tells Isak, "but you don't know anything." In another chilling scene, we see Isak's wife, Karin, freshening up after a tryst, talking sadly to her lover, Isak looking on, untouched.

Tonally, parts of the film are expressed in a bright white light of remembered sunny youth, at the summer house with his young blond cousins; inevitably, I thought of City Slicker Farm. Other parts are lost in harsh shadow, an awaiting darkness, looking into loneliness and the chill of the life he has made for himself, Isak shown forever on the outside looking in. He moves slowly, shuffles along, always in that same long coat, like an actor in a television series consigned to one signature outfit, trapped in it. He is old, but beyond old, burdened by regret. Vision upon vision sweeps over him. In one dream sequence, a stern interrogator questions his professional prowess, critiquing a "surgical masterpiece" Isak has performed: "No pain. Nothing that bleeds or trembles."

"And the punishment?

"I don't know. The usual, I suppose."

"The usual?"

"Loneliness."

Wild Strawberries whispered to me, *You don't want the life you've chosen.* I might lead a good, successful life, like Isak Borg's, only to reach the end of it filled with regret and remorse. Isaac had tasted the sweetness of young love. He'd worked hard, done well, was set to receive a high honor. And yet now, at the end of his Good Life, he was confronted with his failings—hurts caused, opportunities not embraced, kindnesses not extended. In his own mind, he was condemned as lonely and cold. I came away certain that I was destined for this self-same course, Isak Borg's destiny irrevocably mine. I felt *no space* between him and me, my identification with him utter and complete. We were one and the same, his fate was mine unless I did something to alter it.

I was not the only film-goer to appreciate *Wild Strawberries.* It firmly established Bergman's reputation; it was acclaimed by critics, named to numerous best-film lists. But we see many a "best" film that leaves us cold; or that we duly appreciate for a couple of hours and promptly forget. From this film, though, I could never move on. I've watched it every few years since and each time was reduced to tears. No, it is not a film for everyone. It is subtitled from the Swedish, shot in black and white, mostly pretty bleak: A long car drive with a grumpy old man; Isak's lip quivering in existential anguish; the confrontation with his past; the wistful realization that maybe he was better off in his little country medical practice of years past, where the local folk liked and admired him. All this would not touch every viewer. But it did me. And that was the raw, irreducible fact of it. It delivered a terrible truth. It shunted my life off its rails.

A day or two after seeing it, I walked the few blocks to Mt. Vernon Place, planted myself on a park bench, and stewed all day over the film, my life, and my relationship with Bev. I remember nothing of what I said to her the next day when she and I finally talked. Except that I told her I no longer wished to marry her. That we should just be friends. I don't remember whether she cried bitterly, or whether I did, or whether I showed any empathy, understanding, or love. I doubt it.

Whatever compassion I felt for Isak Borg, or myself, after the film's emotional battering, didn't extend to Bev. I simply *decreed*: We weren't getting married and she needed to move out—which she did soon after, to an apartment a few blocks away.

"Please do me one favor," she wrote in the note she left me. "If you change your mind, don't hold out from your ever-lovin' stubbornness. And remember—I love you. I'll be at Ken's tonight & here to pick up my stuff tomorrow."

The emotions the film unleashed in me froze out rational thought or ordinary human kindness. Somehow, in a confused jumble of feeling, I felt—I knew—that our marriage would consign me to a path that led toward Isak Borg's dark, late-in-life regret. Somehow, one, my relationship with Bev, two, marriage itself, and three, the cold, constrained life of the film's fussy old professor had become indivisible, not three separate things, but one. Together they tangled my brain with regret, disappointment, and yes, at age 22, fear of death, a Gordian knot that could be severed only by one savage stroke. That stroke was my pronouncement that we were done as a couple. In the years since, I've struggled for a way to picture my behavior in softer, more forgiving terms, as somehow justified, as not so selfish, unfeeling, or cruel. I've never found one.

It was only later that I came to appreciate what I'd done. At the time and long after, I papered over my conduct with the reminder that, after all, Bev and I remained friends over the next year or two. For the next nine months, we lived around the corner from one another, saw each other occasionally. Later, when I went to Europe, we corresponded regularly: I wrote to her of my loneliness there, she wrote to me of her own troubles, her awful boyfriend, her struggles to overcome her own demons.

A few years later—by that time we were out of touch—she married. She had children. She'd made what I supposed was a good life for herself. Both of us, after all, had been so *young*. Such things *happened*. Then, and in the years before I began this book—and before readers more sensitive than I would react to my story with visible embarrassment—my callous treatment of Bev didn't seem to me quite so irretrievably terrible.

And after all, hadn't I thereby remained true to my new values? I'd busted out of my old life. I'd broken free of deadening constraint. I'd struck a blow for personal liberation. *That,* in the summer of 1968, could seem all that mattered...

⌣

The Sixties had reached down into me.

Later, I'd notice that those born just a few years later than I, in the early and mid-1950s, often had quite a different experience of the time; as teenagers in the late 1960s, their world was imbued from the outset with change, new freedoms, color, and disruption. The Sixties was simply the world into which they'd been pitched, the only world they knew.

But me, I was conceived at the very end of World

War II, about the time of the first atomic bomb and the Japanese surrender. Born in 1946, I was among the first cohort of baby boomers, older than both my siblings and all seven of my first cousins; I had less in common with most of them than with my aunts and uncles, parents and grandparents, whose values had been forged by the Depression and World War II. I was of the post-war generation, yet the war lived in me. I'd read Eisenhower's *Crusade in Europe*, about the military campaigns that culminated in the D-Day landings, when I was 14. On television, I watched *Victory at Sea*, about the naval war in the Pacific, each American victory musically festooned by Richard Rodgers' swelling score. I was the product of what had *just* happened, the events of the recent past, not what was *about* to happen. High school and college had occupied me from 1959 to 1966; but the period we today refer to as the Sixties emerged only toward the end of that period. Up to when I became engaged to Bev, I'd lived something closer to a Fifties life.

Not long ago, a friend of just my age was trying to paint a verbal portrait of himself at the time of his college graduation—how he'd married when he was still 21, got a job as a high school teacher, and immediately had children. His words told a story of clockwork expectation, but his hands told it better: "It was just what you did," he said, holding his two hands rigidly parallel, as if clutching an invisible shoebox between them, and moving it in choppy steps from one side of his body to the other, illustrating the lockstep of those years.

I'd felt that way, too, that as a full-fledged adult, I was to get with the program and gather up life's fruits—college degree, good job, better job, marriage, children, nice house, material pleasures, weekend recreations, the good life, all in smooth and graceful progression. And on the evidence of my first two years in Baltimore, I'd embraced the notion without dissent. Life was what we engineers termed "linear"— rising in an orderly straight line, without unsettling dips, twists, and discontinuities. Even dropping out of the weapons industry had represented but slight disruption: A few fraught months and I had emerged unscathed, ethically cleansed in my own eyes, soon back where I'd been—with good job, good girl, restored to the security and comfort of the ever-upward life.

I could never be the perfect hippie. I could never smoke dope with the blithe assurance that it was about the best thing I could do in my life. The war in Vietnam, and the reaction against it, grew during my young adulthood. I shared the revulsion for it that most of my generation did, yet I could never shed the conviction that sometimes, though rarely, war might be necessary and right; that there were evils in the world that could not be stopped by reaching for a joint or hoisting a picket sign. In this narrow sense, I had been born too early—too early to give myself over unquestioningly to the times.

But now, by July 1968, the times had caught up with me.

I understand today that the Sixties left some people wounded. The relaxation of Fifties proprieties, the dissolution and the drugs, the collapse of long-standing social, sexual, and racial barriers, the ceaseless questioning of all that earlier generations held sacred, the political usurpation of the governing classes by grass-roots movements, the loudness and incivility, the sit-ins and demonstrations, the challenges even to patriotism and filial duty—all these left some feeling anchorless, uncertain, and lost. For them, the Sixties was a ragged black hole in their personal psyches.

Not for me, though. I came to believe then, and believe still, that the Sixties were what the country needed. Certainly they were what I needed. "Throw over the System," those years sang. "Embrace disruption, openness, untrammeled freedom. Challenge the precepts of your parents. Reject the life charted out for you."

I had to grow into the new ideas. Under the mesmeric spell of Bob Dylan's words and music, the Sixties inched up on me, my eyes gradually widening to change and possibility, more slowly than for others, I think—but made all the sweeter by having come up through those earlier, flatter Fifties. There'd been no love beads during my college years, no marijuana highs, no anti-war protests. The Pill had only just begun a sexual revolution. We'd been caught up in a Cold War with the Soviets and never knew when the world would come to a nuclear end, as it almost had during the Cuban Missile Crisis, when I was 16 and a college freshman.

Bland, slide rule-clacking Rensselaer had managed to drain drama and intensity from life, from mine, anyway. I'd inhabited a world of sophomoric silliness—*Playboy* centerfolds, frat party blow-outs, hockey games, and adolescent dreams of the great jobs, sexy sports cars, and willing women waiting for us once we were out of school. Among the suburban and small-town sensibilities and careerist concerns of most of my classmates, a flatness hung over my four years there. Outside of class, I'd hardly read a thing.

Baltimore, in 1966, had felt like a resurrection of the curious boy I'd been before "growing up" in college.

But midway through 1968, bound for marriage and a corporate career, I sensed I was bound for a life of only mild pleasures and modest achievement. Had I thought it out in quite that way? I doubt whether I *thought* at all; I'd become susceptible to the sort of sudden oceanic Truth that had swept down on me that day to deflect me from grad school. Marrying Bev—marrying anyone, really—seemed like an artifact of a bygone time, and of an already alien vestige of myself. It was a different kind of life I wanted, though I couldn't have said what it was.

It was only within the clutch of *Wild Strawberries* that I abruptly knew there was a something-more I needed, and that I had to jump off the train I was on to get it. It wasn't just the film's story line that worked its way into me. It was the film itself, *as* a film, in all its artistry; this I came to see much later, after I'd become a writer. It opened up in me such a well of feeling—so charged, so painful, and yet so extraordinarily beautiful—that the life path awaiting me seemed pallid by contrast.

Maybe Bergman's character was withdrawn or cold, but Bergman's art was impassioned and hot. After so intense an experience at the hands of this consummate artist, how could I consign myself to a decent-enough job, a good- enough marriage? It was as if *Wild Strawberries* had made me unfit for an ordinary life of ordinary equanimity. However tender my feelings for Bev, they ran hard up against an awakened need for something bigger than marriage and "mere" happiness, something worthy of the titanic stakes of the times.

In acting as precipitately as I did, I shed some of the timid, tamped-down part of me I didn't like. And I was pushed onto an alternative path that would lead to new loves, new work, a whole new reading of myself. Given all that was to come, I don't doubt today that splitting up with Bev was what I needed to do. But ironically, in the insensitive way I did it, I was enacting the worst of what Isak Borg's son and daughter-in-law saw in him, and that he, in his terrible dreams, saw in himself. As I write these lines, that's what I think about most, and regret most acutely.

It has not escaped my notice that the book you are reading, composed in my late sixties and early seventies, has confronted me with life regrets, embarrassments, and futilities much as Isak Borg's journey did his. My feelings as I read old letters, as I reflect on the hurt I have caused others, strikingly mirror those of Isak Borg on his way to Lund.

8

Bev moved out. I saw her occasionally that summer, but romantically I was alone. August was the time of the political conventions, the Republicans in Miami, the Democrats in Chicago. Bobby Kennedy was dead. Hubert Humphrey, the vice-president, was gunning for the Democratic nomination, but the upstart, Eugene McCarthy, the upright, moral voice, antagonistic to the war from the beginning, was still in it. For a time that summer, I worked for McCarthy; I was "clean for Gene"—the phrase embraced back then for presumably ill-kempt hippies willing to tidy themselves up to work on his campaign. Mornings, before work, I'd hand out McCarthy fliers at the Bendix parking lot. And when McCarthy arrived at the Baltimore airport, I was there, snapping pictures of the country's last best hope for peace. At the Chicago convention in the last week of August, 6,000 Federal troops and 18,000 National Guards, together with Mayor Daley's cops, tangled with protesters outside, while inside, Hubert Humphrey, Johnson's man, beat McCarthy on the first ballot.

On the job, I'd started to worry about the safety of the company's speed control system, now coming off the assembly line at Quad Avenue. By my reckoning, blockage of one recalcitrant valve, controlled by a five-cent part, could leave the throttle stuck full on; the engine would rev uncontrollably, neither a tap on the brake pedal nor a pulse from its electronics able to rein it in, the car roaring ahead until it crashed. I did my best to alert my colleagues to the danger, and got leave to work on an electromechanical fix. And so, the next few months after *Wild Strawberries* churned on. I went to work. I fenced in a few tournaments. I took some nice pictures and enjoyed my darkroom. I bought a 35mm camera, with a bunch of lenses, to supplement the twin-lens reflexes I'd been using all along. In October, I took it down to Fells Point, Baltimore's old waterfront neighborhood, to record its first "Fun Festival," taking impromptu pictures of babies and grizzled old men.

On November 5, Nixon was elected president.

At 5:30 a.m. on November 20, an underground explosion rocked a coal mine in West Virginia. Smoke and flames shot 150 feet from the mouth of the Llewelyn shaft of the Consol No. 9 mine; a motel clerk twelve miles away felt it. In the next few hours, 21 miners managed to escape. Seventy-eight did not, and were trapped underground. They were presumed dead, but no one could say for sure. Someone would later call it the first nationally televised mine disaster. The big decision was whether to seal the mine, smothering the underground fires, and so consign the men to certain death. Or else, in a final, probably futile gesture, against all the evidence of the poisoned underground air, keep trying to reach them.

I don't recall viewing TV coverage of the disaster or newspaper accounts of it, though I must have. On Thanksgiving day, I got into my car and drove 250 miles over and through the wrinkled mountain ridges of western Maryland to West Virginia. I remained there a few days, with the newspaper and television reporters, the coal company officers, and the grief-stricken families anxiously awaiting news of their fathers and brothers. I attended news conferences. I talked with family members. And I was there when, nine days after the explosion, with samples of air within the mine all coming back as lethally poisonous, John Corcoran, president of Consolidated Coal, announced that the mine was to be sealed, entombing the miners. I took pictures of the aggrieved family members, the hardscrabble buildings, the Red Cross trucks, the bare company stores, the mine portals. "Thru These Portals Pass the Finest Coal Miners in the World," one sign read. Before I was through, I wrote an account datelined "Fairmont, West Virginia—November 29," which I ended with the time-honored newspaper symbol, "30."

My story was poorly written, rife with generalities, deficient in particulars, bad in every way. But I wrote it out by hand—in schoolboy print, so at least it would be legible—and sent it off to the *Village Voice*, the New York newspaper most apt to be receptive, I imagined, to its criticism of the mine owners and the union alike. I see no need to embarrass myself by quoting from it here, even briefly. The *Voice* wrote back to say they couldn't use it and were kind enough not to comment further.

None of my actions that Thanksgiving, midway through my 23rd year, follow intelligibly from the life I led at the time. To simply pick up on a whim and go somewhere hundreds of miles away, least of all the mountains of West Virginia, was out of character. I wasn't between jobs. I wasn't fleeing a bad love affair. I wasn't on drugs. I had no particular affinity or personal tie to miners, or coal, or West Virginia, nor anything beyond conventional liberal sympathy for the injustices visited on working people. Later, trying to reconstruct my motivation, I couldn't.

No one could be more skeptical than I to claims of fate or karma; I don't believe in any of that now and I didn't then. But the West Virginia trip baffles me and, if I didn't know any better, and could relax my skepticism for even a moment, I might be led to think its sole purpose was to propel me through trains of coincidence and circumstance into the arms of Maura McNair.

Back in April, distracted by a flickering dashboard

light, I'd rammed my yellow Spitfire into a parked car. I borrowed money from my dad to get it fixed, then promptly unloaded the jinxed, unlucky thing. It had been fun, when it wasn't conking out, and when the windshield wiper wiped, but I'd gotten my adolescent fill of sports cars and now went the other way entirely.

My grandfather, nearing 80, had decided to give up driving. His car devolved on me, and I was happy to get it. It was a black 1954 Chrysler New Yorker Deluxe, one step down from an Imperial, black and chrome outside, bordello red leather inside, that had been housed in the garage of our two-family house in Brooklyn. As a middle-teen, I'd sometimes swing up the garage door, squeeze through the narrow space between the wall and the car door, slip into the driver's seat and just sit there, enjoying the quiet, soaking up the dusky smell of the red leather, sitting there alone, content.

Cars from 1954 boasted chrome, lots of it, utilitarian and ornamental, bumpers and doodads, every bit of hardware possible meant to glisten and shine. But my grandfather's car had chrome where no one else's did. His and my dad's small company did every sort of electroplating—zinc and cadmium, nickel and brass, and chromium, too. So one day Grandpa, in his inimitable way, had several thick, heavy bars of copper bent into the appropriate shape, electroplated with bright chrome, and attached to the car as supplemental bumpers. They were chrome like any chrome, but instead of thin sheet metal beneath the gleam, it was solid copper; his Chrysler was one of a kind. And after lousy driving and sporadic maintenance had run my Spitfire into the ground such that I had to get rid of it, I was pleased to have this family heirloom.

This was the car I now was driving back to Baltimore. But 75 miles into the return trip, heading back east through the mountains again, it protested. For its 14 years, Grandpa's car had low mileage. But time alone, not just mileage, takes its mechanical toll, and it had never been tested in country like this. West Virginia was all hills, hollows, and mountain scenery. It had scant agriculture; little of it was level enough to farm.

Coal, buried in the ancient hills, was king, and the hills never abated; this was before the Interstates had smoothed out the ups and downs. It was up one impossible grade, cresting the hill, a spectacular drop down the next slope, then up the next. Hills, steep and steeper, mile after mile, scarcely a level stretch all along route 310 from Mannington, and then route 50 through West Virginia, and then Maryland briefly, back into West Virginia. If you had a stick shift, you were constantly down-shifting; with an automatic, as mine was, the transmission was forever *working*, feeling the engine strain, shifting down. And now, finally, Grandpa's transmission began to grumble.

Soon, it was all glurks and hesitations and scrunches until finally, with a stink of oil and a gasp of smoke, the car died, coming to rest, finally, by the side of a road in the middle of nowhere. This was no time for acting out the age-old male ritual of lifting the hood, peering in, fiddling with a valve or connection and magically getting the thing to work. I didn't know that much about cars, but I knew enough to realize that would be futile. It was the old car's transmission, badly beaten up by the hills, that had burned out; that was plain enough. There was nothing I could do.

I hitched a ride into the nearest town, Mt. Storm, West Virginia, population about a hundred. There I was deposited at an antique service station, complete with pot-bellied coal stove, and left to the tender mercies of Mr. Shanholtz, a middle-aged, crew-cut man who oozed sly intelligence. He and his assistant, who maybe was his father, towed Grandpa's car some miles back to the station. When he lifted the hood and started poking around, I snapped some pictures, just to do something; here, out in the wilds of West Virginia, 200 miles from such civilization as could be found in Baltimore and Washington, D.C., Mt. Storm felt as alien as an Amazon jungle. From all I could make out, Mr. Shanholtz was American, but so thick was his back-country accent, I could scarcely understand him.

He knew he had me good. I was a kid, I was alone,

I didn't know anything. What was I going to do, have the car towed back to Baltimore? Or leave it here with him to replace the transmission of a 14-year-old car and then, weeks later, somehow get back here to retrieve it? Mr. Shanholtz might never realize my chrome-bumpered car was like no other in the world. But he made me an offer he probably knew I couldn't refuse—fifty bucks to take the thing off my hands. Pretty soon, with $8.70 of it going for a bus ticket, I was on a Greyhound bus for Baltimore.

Back in Baltimore, I took the next couple of days off to look for a car. I found a red '66 VW Beetle, talked to its seller on the phone, scribbling the key information on the back of a business card. We arranged to meet so I could see and test-drive it. She was leaving for Europe and needed to sell.

There was insurance to work out and an inspection, but finally, after several meetings and phone conversations, all of them somehow more interesting than they had any reason to be, the deal was done. We decided to meet over dinner at Jimmy Wu's, a Chinese restaurant and long-standing Baltimore institution, all fortune cookies and chow mein. It wasn't long into our wonton soups that I asked if I could sleep with her.

She didn't skip a beat, just looked at me, steady: "Do you know...how old I am?"

I didn't know how old she was, but she was stunning, with high cheekbones, long, flaming red hair, and a deep, throaty voice no doubt made more seductive by the cigarettes she was always smoking. Her name was Esther, she was 41, divorced, lived in a small, top-floor apartment on Bolton Street. She worked as a chemist in a laboratory at Johns Hopkins, but was leaving the States at the end of the month for a job in Leiden, in the Netherlands. She was formidably well-read. Over the next few weeks, she introduced me to the French writer Celine, gave me a paperback copy of a quirky cult novel about a callow prep school boy and his *Hundred Dollar Misunderstanding* with a prostitute. We had long talks about everything, and spent Christmas day together in Washington, where we had dinner at a downtown hotel.

One day as the calendar ground toward the new year, I was at Esther's when she got a call, answered it briefly, and told me a friend was coming over. We were still in bed when the doorbell rang. Esther got up to let her in. I stayed under the covers, looking on. Her friend breezed in, wearing a little patchwork jacket, talking a mile a minute. She didn't stay long, just long enough to inject the room with energy and light. Her name was Maura, she was in her twenties, and she was a Ph.D. student in biology.

A few days later, on the 28th, her apartment packed up, her red VW now mine, Esther boarded a plane for Europe. But before she left, she said she needed to tell me one more thing: She wanted me to get to know this Maura. She said it tenderly but with urgency, as if it were a command, or a blessing.

9

Not long ago, I had lunch with Jay, my old boss from the Ammo Lab, my first job in Baltimore. He was in his eighties now and we hadn't seen each other for many a year. Over Indian food at a table set beside a sun-filled window at a restaurant close enough I could walk to, we recalled people we'd known back then. We talked of the later history of the Ammo Lab, after I'd left; of his dinners with old cronies; of how the old outdoor firing range was now, impossibly, a Walmart. Jay was intelligent, easy enough to talk with, and I appreciated my time with him. Leaving the restaurant, I felt replanted in the soil of my young adulthood.

But as I walked down Canterbury Road, and ambled home along the brick walkways of the Homewood campus, my thoughts winged away from Jay, toward Maura. The two of them had never met; they hadn't even quite overlapped in my life; I'd left the Ammo Lab a year and a half before I met her. But lunch had reminded me, uneasily, of the young man I'd been then. Jay and I had talked. I'd contributed my share. But I'd "managed" our conversation, too, remaining distanced, appropriate, careful, and cool, none of which I could manage for long in the company of Maura McNair.

Almost from the moment I met her, from the moment she began to speak, I was entangled in her life, caught up in her enthusiasms, ideas, resentments, and delights. There was no screen around her. She stood bare, revealed. As she spoke of her troubles in the lab, the awfulness of the war, her unforgiving mother, her friends and enemies, a bridge's beauty, folk dancing, all the things, the many things, the plenitude of things, she cared so deeply about, rattling on, her face aglow, or else shaking her head in mock horror at what she caught herself saying, any vestigial screen vanished, and I was drawn into her, not just understanding but caring, caring about whatever it was, it didn't matter, it mattered only that it mattered to Maura, and so it mattered to me.

I was the best audience she could have hoped for. Sometimes, with colleagues at work, even with friends, I could be inwardly dismissive, only half-present. But with Maura I shed all skepticism, listened in rapt wonder, my mind and heart her possession. Almost from the instant she whirled into Esther's apartment, wearing her little patchwork jacket, running over, afire, I loved her. I became a different man, the man who loved Maura.

A couple of weeks after Esther left, early in 1969,

I got a letter from her in the Netherlands. Her new lab was a new world. She'd seen so much. And yet she resented the light repartee into which she fell with her new colleagues, the absence of intimate conversation. She spoke of the ease with which she and I had talked during our brief time together, gesture and body language filling in for failed words. We lacked that now. "Now, when I would really like to communicate with you, I am painfully aware of this and self-conscious as a result. If you write and tell me more of who you are, I would be very happy!" She signed the letter and sealed it.

But moments later, she wrote again, this second letter reprising her final words to me in Baltimore: "As I ended the letter to you, I recalled this: Get in touch with Maura." She gave me her phone numbers at home and at the lab. "I feel close to both of you in different respects and believe there is a good chance you will like each other. Anything else I could say seems sticky."

I obeyed. Or that, anyway, might be the word to use given how promptly I did as she said. Esther was much older than I. She had advice for me, offered earnestly, with kindness. I listened. It was mid-January when I got Esther's letters. A few days later, I called Maura McNair.

She lived on Druid Hill Lake Drive, across the road from the reservoir in Druid Hill Park, in the middle of Baltimore. A few white people still lived there then, including Maura and a couple of other poor graduate students in a house facing the park. I parked the VW beside the iron-barred reservoir fence, ran across the wide street to her house, and rang the bell. I don't remember much from the rest of the day, except for that moment when, separately, we each got into our own cars, which happened to be parked near one another by the fence. It was like we were saying good-bye for just the few minutes it would take to drive to our destination, a concert at the Baltimore Museum of Art. As Maura turned to me at that last instant before ducking into her car, her face was as I'd remember it always—lit, luminous.

Later, we must have found time to talk of Esther. She and Maura were close friends, I the newcomer. But I think I felt entitled to speak of her because she'd anointed me fit company for Maura; had she not done just that? I think Maura felt it, too. In those first weeks of our relationship, she and I were together almost every day, in and out of each other's lives, and from almost the beginning, in and out of each other's beds. Her body was a rapture. Her mind was a crackling fire of enthusiasms, declamations, and rants. She was unlike anyone I'd ever known.

I always thought of her as tall, and so would sometimes be taken aback to see her standing beside others, or in photos, and realize she was of only average height. But she stood so tall and straight. I took a picture of her much later, after we'd driven across the country to California, beside a Spanish-American War memorial in Sacramento. The sculptor aimed to invest his figure, a soldier with a rifle, with dignity and grace. But Maura, in her short flowered summer dress, wearing her big sunglasses, turned easily toward the camera, embodied so much more of both.

Her face seemed ever to reveal her inner state. When she was happy or excited, it shone. When she was depressed, a recurrent problem for her, the light went out and her face became a death mask. She had stunning green eyes. Her lips were thin. Just sitting, silent, listening, which didn't come easily to her, she could seem imperious, a disapproving queen. That the same face could reveal such wicked delight astonished me.

She was older than I; later I found meaning, or *something,* in the difference in our ages, which was four years, four months, and four days. To me, and almost from the start, everything about Maura seemed endowed with meaning, even when, rationally speaking, I knew it wasn't. She was a fellow New Yorker, grown up across the Narrows in Staten Island. That was enough to make her exotic to me. She was the first Staten Islander I'd ever met, a white Protestant in multi-ethnic New York, the daughter of immigrants from Scotland. Her mother, Grace, brought her up alone after her husband abandoned them following Pearl Harbor.

Mrs. McNair worked in a factory, tending machines that made embroidered garment labels. She spoke with the thick brogue of her native Ayrshire, near Glasgow. She was not, I'd see up close later, warm, expressive, or nurturing. To hear Maura tell it, she'd once threatened to leave her, her own little girl, right there on the street, if she didn't behave. Astonishingly, through intelligence, spirit, and will, Maura emerged from the little house where she'd grown up with her steel-ribbed mother, attended the local high school, then Hunter College in Manhattan, graduating with a named departmental award, and got accepted to one of the most prestigious science graduate programs in the country, at Johns Hopkins.

She wanted to know why the sky was blue, she said; that was science for her at the beginning. That first spring, she took me to Sherwood Gardens for an afternoon among its acres of tulips and azaleas. She walked us around the tulip beds pointing out their nearly invisible variations, discerning differences in fields of color that to me seemed all the same. She loved the living world; that was why she wanted to be a biologist.

But now six years into her Ph. D. program, she wasn't studying living things anymore, or not directly, anyway. Biology, *circa* 1969, meant molecular biology, that transcendence wrought by James Watson and Francis Crick in the early 1950s when they discovered the structure of DNA. The DNA molecule expressed in its very structure the vast range of life in the animal and plant kingdoms, including the numberless variations among those tulips.

Maura was studying variations in rabbit hemoglobin, which by now had begun to pall for her. Still, in the weeks and months after we met, she summoned up enough of her early enthusiasm to thrill me to her science's most basic principles—of how proteins were built from amino acids, and how these were "coded" in the base pairs of DNA's double helix. Here was a genetic code, bearing the very secret of life! I hadn't studied biology past high school, which was before Watson and Crick had walked off with their Nobel Prizes; the only biology I knew was cutting up frogs and memorizing the names of organelles. This new biology was different. But I had enough of a bent for science that, through Maura's beguiling explanations, I became a believer.

Until I met Maura, science for me was simply a tool. Engineers needed it. So did doctors. In school, you learned whatever science you needed in order to "use" it. But for Maura, science was finding things out for the sake of... finding things out, learning how nature worked, discovering something no one had known before. Only once others had confirmed it would it wind up in a book. Government support for basic research left scientists free to explore whatever they wanted, regardless of how relevant, or irrelevant, it seemed—because some of it was sure to yield new drugs, new cures, new technologies. The payoff might not come for decades. But in the meantime, researchers could do as they wished, driven by their curiosity and wonder. Or because it was fun, or yes, sometimes for the sheer glory of getting there first. All this was new to me, and thrilling.

But Maura's life in science, as I got wisps of it now and would see more later, wasn't just experiments, papers, and data, but its own social and communal world. There, in the rarefied community of the lab, were friendships, rivalries, and unabashed ambitions, lab parties and mid-experiment pizza forays, gossip traded beside the ultracentrifuge, competition for equipment and for the lab director's attention, young love, deep-lying resentments, and festering bitterness.

A grad student at a high-octane place like Hopkins was something like a vassal to her lord, there to do her advisor's bidding, staying up till all hours doing experiments that would yield findings she hoped would earn her a degree...but often not *quite* yet. Because first your service was owed the lab director and *his* work. Maura had arrived at Hopkins almost six years before I met her, and was still not near to finishing. She'd had a hard time of it.

In the depths of depression the year before, Maura told me, she had killed herself; that's what she said— not that she'd *tried*, but that she had actually done it, all but succeeding, coming as close to death as you could without being dead, only to be pulled back, finally, from the brink. She'd served a spell at the Phipps, Hopkins's famous psychiatric clinic, where Zelda Fitzgerald had stayed; when *Zelda*, Nancy Milford's biography of F. Scott Fitzgerald's wife, came out the following year, Maura had me read it. Now, more than a year later, she was better but discouraged, often depressed, barely hanging on.

I became more embroiled in her emotional life later. But even now, I was hearing about this thing called "depression," which I was given to understand didn't mean just being unhappy for a day or two. This was new territory I'd never had reason to explore. But Maura's awful experience of being brought back from the dead and her hospitalization were still for me more storied than real, maybe the way combat can seem for untested teenaged soldiers—dangerous and grown up. For now, Maura was boundlessly alive beside me, healthy, young and beautiful, her troubled past a dark jewel in the tiara of her confounding mystery and allure.

A year or so before I'd met her, Maura told me, she had attended a big scientific conference with Friedrich, her doctoral advisor, and slept with him. Friedrich was much older and married. Their relationship, we'd say today, was distorted by a troubling imbalance of power. Yet that's not what imprinted itself on me. It was rather how their sexual couplings stood so near their intellectual life—enzymes, peptides, and N-terminals during the day, in each other's arms at night. The scene—and it *was* a scene, alive in my erotic imagination—exerted a powerful hold on me. It was more than mere jealousy. I couldn't get it out of my head. Because I wanted just *that* for myself, the intimate melding of lust and intellect, the two inextricably bound, sex and brainy communion, together. It was everything I wanted.

To all appearances, of course, one might simply report that, during our first months together, Maura and I "dated." We saw Ingmar Bergman's frightening war movie, *Shame.* We attended Nina Simone and Judy Collins concerts, took in some weird, wholly unmemorable multi-media event at the Peabody Conservatory. We heard Rostropovich play Haydn and Beethoven. We had dinner at Maura's house, pizza at Testani's, the grad student hangout near Hopkins Hospital.

I met some of her friends, fellow grad students. Like Jason, never seen to fret, somehow above the usual grad student angst and grunge. And Rita, from Texas, in her easy-going maturity a foil to her deliciously neurotic, super-intellectual husband Howard. Maura had become friends with some black children near her apartment, and one time we picked up Vivian, about 11, and Joey, her adorable kid brother, and spent the day with them. During this period, I was as active as ever in photography and when the local camera club scheduled a harbor cruise one weekend, Maura and I went. I made one picture of a constellation of black birds against the white sky. Later, in the dark room, I'd heighten the contrast to form a study in black and white that, in its stark, lonely beauty, would mean Maura to me once she left for Europe.

For by March it was plain that, like Esther four months before, Maura was bound for Europe. Friedrich had returned to Germany. Maura was his student. She was doing experiments that served him; he needed her. And she, of course, needed him. If she wanted her degree, she would have to join him there, at the Max Planck Institute in Göttingen, a medieval college town in central West Germany. In mid-April, Maura was to get on a plane and leave.

I drove her to the airport. Today it's known as Baltimore-Washington International, but then, much smaller, it was called Friendship Airport, named for a Methodist church on whose land it was built. We took photos of one another, taking turns perched on a vinyl waiting room chair, both of us looking way too serious, or else just miserable. The better one of me shows me at 22, with dark hair, long sideburns, puffing on a cigarette. Propped on the arm of the chair while Maura snapped the picture is what looks like a boxed gift, strung tight with cord. It was no gift, of course, but Maura's thesis, or rather a draft of the parts of it she had finished, with notes, papers and experimental results. It was the most precious thing she had. It wasn't going with the checked luggage; it would never leave her side.

We kissed good-bye. I had known her for three months. I scarcely knew her.

10

"I started missing you the minute the plane started its engines," Maura wrote soon after arriving in Göttingen. From the first day, she'd been overwhelmed by the language barrier, German all around her. She felt helpless. It was cold. She was cold. "It was snowing yesterday and it was very odd to see the tulips and hyacinths and all the other spring flowers here nestled in snow."

Some buildings in town, which the war had left mostly untouched, went back to the 13th century. Everything, Maura reported, was astonishingly clean. The lab was modern and spacious, people working day and night. She told of venturing into town looking for food. Bratwurst was about all she recognized, so that's what she got, with French fries she could only point to. "I won't starve because I can order at least that." Later, she, Friedrich, and his family went for a drive an hour east of town into the Harz mountains with their picture-postcard villages.

Maura's letters to me always looked the same—blue-tinted Luftpost envelopes, bright blue and red slashes along the edges, anointed by Deutsche Bundespost stamps, their Germanness sounding an extra bass note. The backs were imprinted, in modernist sans-serif CAPITAL letters, MAX-PLANCK-INSTITUT

FUR EXPERIMENTELLE MEDIZIN, ABTEILLUNG MOLEKULARE BIOLOGIE; in the bit of space remaining, "M. McNair" managed to squeeze in her name. From Greta in Guatemala, I'd gotten a few letters covered with colorful foreign stamps. But these more sedate envelopes from Germany, addressed to me in flowing cursive across the front, Maura's heart waiting for me within, soon had me conditioned to Pavlovian perfection.

In our few months together in Baltimore, some alchemical magic had worked a lifelong change in me, leaving me alive to all Maura thought, felt, and did. I looked up to her as role model and heroine. Except for Canada, I'd never been out of the country. Maura had almost instantly remodeled herself into a world traveler; her letters and postcards told of freely slipping off to Berlin or Rome. I was an engineer in a big, boring American company, my energies devoted to trifles of consumer desire, while Maura, in Europe, consorted with the best scientific minds in the world. She was more experienced than I in every way, had tasted emotional depths I could only imagine. I was a rank innocent, just a few years and a few women out of my overlong virginity; Maura was a woman of the world, scampering into bed with Herr Professor Doktor Friedrich, mostly enjoying the wolf whistles men in Rome shot her way. Back in Göttingen, she'd write, she was "simpatico" with Nagaraj, one of the post docs; I didn't even know what "simpatico" *meant.*

And why did she invariably call Alessandro, another lab partner, the seemingly more intimate "Sandro"? I didn't know whether she slept with him, or Friedrich, or anyone else over there. But jealous and threatened I was, there in Maura's shadow.

If Maura sensed any of this, she never let on. In her letters, she made it seem she loved and longed for me. She sent me small gifts. In an early Bob Dylan song, "Boots of Spanish Leather," the narrator tells how his girl, off to Europe, asks what he might want from her as a gift. Only her love and safe return, he says. By song's end she makes him realize she's got more on her mind than him. But in her scores of letters across these months, Maura wasn't like that. She didn't hold back. She wrote often and lovingly. But however often and however lovingly, I, back in Baltimore, could find no composure. My mind was in too many pieces.

My relationship with Bev Shorr had been easy and familiar; true, I'd somehow refashioned that into a vice, a recipe for too small a life. Now, with Maura, it was all quite the other way; all she was, did, said, and thought challenged me. That she was a gentile from working-class Protestant roots and I a middle-class Jew was the least of it. I was more optimistic, tending to tolerate the foolishness, injustice, and mean-spiritedness of the world; she was left angered and hurt by it. If Bev coddled me, Maura unsettled me, holding out her hand, pulling me along an unfamiliar path toward a new me.

In early May, a few weeks after arriving in Germany, Maura wrote me about my efforts at international folk dancing, which she'd introduced me to in Baltimore and I'd tried again, miserably, after she left. "Your feelings at folk dancing are the ones you are going to feel everywhere—that's you!! And you go where you go." I should try once more, it was fun, a way to "challenge yourself to learn something even at the cost of feeling clumsy, inadequate, and foolish."

Inevitably, during our first months together, we'd compared notes on music. I liked Dylan, Simon & Garfunkel, folk music, Broadway show tunes, had a peculiar un-counterculturish weakness for Frank Sinatra. Maura liked Janis Joplin and the Rolling Stones; we debated endlessly whether "I Can't Get No Satisfaction" was great music or, with its incessantly repeated refrain, noise.

She loved classical music, felt a special affinity for Ravel's haunting *Pavane for a Dead Princess*. For me, Maura *became* the dead princess; I'd listen to the record, hanging on every mournful chord, imagining myself brought ineffably close to her. Maura, who was taking cello lessons at the time, took me to my first classical concert. I landed comfortably in this new musical landscape; it was no threat. As Maura offered enthusiastic introductions and informed opinions, I lapped them up, easily and permanently.

But it was not folk music Maura was urging on

me now, but folk *dancing.*

⌣‾‾‾‾

It must have been in fifth grade, one day toward the end of the school year, when I felt the air in the room change. Whatever we were supposed to be doing at our gouged, old wooden desks, our attention focused on the book in front of us or else on Mrs. Coughlin at the front, suddenly we weren't; the taut lines of the classroom had abruptly relaxed. To my left, toward the ceiling-high windows, some of my classmates had risen from their seats and, chattering away, were moving things around, upending the room, clearing space. Someone had brought in a portable phonograph. A record was spinning, scratchy music pouring out of it. Some of my classmates, both boys and girls, were dancing. I had not known this was in the works. I don't remember Mrs. Coughlin or anyone else saying it was time, or giving instruction. It just happened. The music played and the other kids my age or a little older were up, out of their seats, happy, loose, and wriggling to the music.

Where'd they learn that? How did this happen? Where had I been? They're only kids, like me, but they're dancing. Like grown-ups. It wasn't just that they knew how to dance and I didn't. They'd learned without my realizing it, as if behind my back. Or else, they'd always known, known all the steps, all the tunes.

This magical thinking was bad enough, but I made it worse: I didn't say, "Everybody else has learned, and so will I." Rather, I drew the fatally wrong conclusion—that from dancing I was forever excluded. I'd been condemned to another class or category, of non-dancers: It wasn't that I *didn't* or *couldn't*. It was that I *wasn't*—a dancer.

During the 1950s, under the aegis of Dick Clark—"America's teenager," they called him later—*American Bandstand* was *the* popular dance show. Teenaged boys in grown-up jackets and ties and girls in skirts and bobby sox danced their little hearts out to Jerry and the Juniors, or whoever was the current heartthrob. The camera barely budged, just let bodies jounce and bounce in front of the lens. All in black and white. Sometimes the singer of a hit song would show up to lip-synch his or her rock masterpiece.

What I never did was simply plunk myself down on the floor opposite the TV, or on our very Fifties sofa, and watch *American Bandstand*. Rather, with Mom shopping, or busy in the kitchen, or upstairs with my grandmother, I'd flip the channel to it and, for a few uneasy minutes, sneak a look. This would be after school, when I was still at P.S. 203 or else a little later, in junior high, age 11 or 12. I was not watching, exactly, but peeking, guiltily, with the lively sense that I shouldn't be doing it.

Today, I can imagine others of *Bandstand's*

millions of adolescent viewers getting up to dance at home, imitating dance moves, giving themselves over to it, inviting friends over to dance together. I didn't. I was always alone. I never tried the steps. It was as if I'd been left permanently outside, looking through a window at an illicit scene—silent, scarcely breathing, mouth gone dry. Sounds like pornography? Except that this was the most popular show on TV for kids my age.

My parents had nothing against television; we watched like everyone else. *Gunsmoke,* and *What's My Line,* and *Bilko,* and *You Are There* with Walter Cronkite, which took you back to the Crusades or the French Revolution, or *Your Show of Shows* with Sid Caesar. I suppose those programs enjoyed a kind of parental *imprimatur.* The big-boned *Gunsmoke* hero, Matt Dillon, embodied healthy grown-up values. *What's My Line,* with Bennett Cerf and Broadway actress Arlene Francis, boasted just the sort of sophisticated repartee my mom loved. And when the hero of *Have Gun Will Travel,* Paladin, wasn't putting away bad guys, he would spout Shakespeare; my parents ate it up. As for Brooklyn bus driver Ralph Kramden of *The Honeymooners* and his loose-limbed friend from the sewers, Ed Norton—well, they were sheer genius.

So popular entertainment wasn't banned from the house. But one way or another, it had to be *smart*—clever, quick, or deep. And *Bandstand,* as I saw it through my parents' eyes, was none of those, just brainless teenagers brainlessly gyrating to brainless music.

My folks weren't big dancers themselves and didn't go out dancing Friday nights, as some other couples of their generation did. I did see them take to the floor occasionally at weddings or bar mitzvahs; my father seemed awkward, but managed to look like he was having a good time. They never encouraged me to try it, however, or to take lessons—never suggested it might be a socially smart thing to do. I suspect they'd have denied having anything against dancing. But they had nothing to say in its favor, either—nothing to say, period. It wasn't *important* to them.

In our house, words, acts, and ideas were not uncritically right or wrong; there was plenty of room for grays and gradations, which we could discuss freely. But important versus not-important? That seemed more black and white: Some parts of life had weight and worth, others you could ignore. I didn't need to be told there was something irrelevant about dancing; to them, I intuited, getting up to dance, just to do it, just to be part of things, just to hold your partner close and breathe her fragrance, just for the sake of a simple, stupid-assed good time of it away from grownups and grownup seriousness, maybe along the way becoming graceful, wasn't us. I needed no sniggers or lifted eyebrows to get the message: It wasn't important to them, so it wasn't important.

In my addled adolescent consciousness, watching *Bandstand* was a betrayal of my parents' values.

And so later, at a party, in college, or anytime, really, when the dancing started, I stopped. Abruptly, I'd turn quite still. Even at City Slicker, for Friday night square dancing, even with Cathy and Jan urging me on, I couldn't move. Over the years, women determined to dance with me made the same claims—that they weren't much good as dancers themselves, that they felt self-conscious, too, that nobody cared what you looked like, that all you needed was to get out there and move to the music. This never worked with me. Nobody could shake me. 1. The music started up. 2. Couples migrated to the dance floor. The two together, like one of those two-part household epoxies that together create an unbreakable bond, rendered me immobile.

Then I met Maura, who every week went to Levering Hall on the Hopkins campus for "international folk dancing." This was not square dancing, English country dancing, or contra dancing, but line and circle dancing to the haunting, hypnotic rhythms of Greek, Balkan, and Middle Eastern music. It was beautiful to behold, the long snaking lines of dancers, many wearing knitted belts, peasant vests, and sandals from the folk dancing countries, all grace and sinuosity. It wasn't rock, wasn't the jitterbug, wasn't the cha-cha, wasn't the twist, wasn't any dancing I'd thought to try, wasn't *Bandstand*. So maybe it wouldn't be so freighted with old baggage? But it was. Maura took me to Levering, urged me to try it. I did get up once or twice, fumbling ineptly, and almost immediately retreated to the side—where I remained, silent, unmoving, *still.*

That was before she left. Once she was in Germany, I resolved to try it again on my own, but managed no better. I stayed to the side, watching itself an agony, returned home, transmuted my bitterness into words, and wrote Maura. "The longer you stay on the sidelines," she wrote back, "the more difficult it gets to join in—and the more depressed you'll get. God, how I would love to dance with you."

———

In mid-May, I took a brief vacation, alone, a road trip into the south. I'd grown up gorged with tales of the South's unrepentant anti-Semitism. And any fitful attention I gave the civil rights movement had only added to its horrific mystery. In Virginia, I crashed a fraternity party. In Atlanta, I stayed at the downtown Y, spent an easy afternoon in the park with a blond German hippie girl. But I learned little about the alien south, for I couldn't stop thinking of Maura. In an Italian restaurant off Peachtree Street, I asked the waitress for pen and paper and wrote Maura a long letter. It was hopelessly abstract, incoherent, really, and I didn't send it, which was smart.

Back at Bendix, it could have seemed that everything was fine. A year and a half there and I was still working on the speed control, looking into a fix for what I conceived as its safety issues, and preparing drawings for a prototype sensor housing I thought might resolve its tolerance accumulation problem. Then, about a month after Maura's departure, I was asked to join the advanced concepts team, a sort of poor man's R & D group. This was good; in the Bendix engineering cosmos, it ranked as a modest laurel. But by now I had scant respect for anything we built. The work itself was often interesting but the products themselves seemed stupid and trivial— especially set against the war, which made everything else seem trivial.

My work didn't contribute to America's war. And I was safe from being dragged into it myself. But I still hated it. Back in October, before I met Maura, George Wallace, the former governor of Alabama and a virulent segregationist, brought his populist road show to Baltimore, part of a third-party presidential bid that would net him ten million votes and five southern states in November. He was a malevolent yet entertaining public figure, and when he came to the Baltimore Civic Center to pump up his flock of followers, I was there to see him. There were plenty of hecklers on hand for him, too. I had my Nikkormat and took pictures. The hard part was when they played the national anthem and, against the backdrop of Wallace's twisted, empty-headed xenophobia, I simply could not rise for it. The war was sickness, curse, and horror and the United States of America, my country, was its perpetrator.

I felt a mounting revulsion. Part of me just wanted *out*, out of America. Protected by my 2A, I didn't *need* to emigrate to Canada, but now I began to think I would anyway, that "our northern neighbor" was simply a better, more peaceable place. Exiting my defense job after the Pentagon march in 1967, I'd come close to leaving. Now, a year and a half later, I considered it again. One colleague in my new job was a French-Canadian with whom I'd sometimes exchange a few words of French. I visited the Baltimore office of the American Friends Service Committee, the Quaker group that helped anti-war Americans get to Canada. I wrote Maura, laying out my thoughts about leaving Bendix, and America. "I understand your wanting to find a very new place—to find a new you," she wrote back. "No, you shouldn't stay at the Bendix mill. This is destroying you."

Canada, and Montreal, beckoned. I began taking French lessons from Laure, the wife of a Hopkins grad student. There was nothing uncertain or ambiguous about any of this. The logic was clear: Brush up on my French. Leave Bendix. Leave America. Wake up in Montreal.

And then the tectonic plates shifted.

"I feel very confused," Maura wrote me. She'd

argued with Friedrich about a paper she was writing. They couldn't agree on what her experiments really meant; he wanted her to draw conclusions from them she thought unfounded. Talking with other grad students and postdocs left her feeling only more exhausted, dispirited, and apart. And she didn't know what to make of my letters, which probably seemed vague, and certainly offered no relief from the pressure on her. She wanted out, too.

> I am very overwhelmed by Europe. I think of it as a neighborhood and I want to explore it. Did you know there is a <u>bus</u> that leaves every week from Munich to India?! Going through Bulgaria, Rumania, Turkey, etc. etc. All those exotic places—How they excite me. I want to tell you—Stop! Come here, let's just live. Fuck everything else. Fuck the system. Fuck the Plan—No aims, no goals, just living free and as we want. I wonder if that's possible. Can anyone really be free? Does life really need a plan? Or is it all an escapist dream?

She lamented that the photos she had of me, probably the ones we'd taken at Friendship Airport that time, made me look too serious. "To take this life seriously is stupid," she went on.

It would mean that you really believed that there

was a purpose to it and rules to be played by. There isn't. We make them, or more accurately our ancestors have made them for us...

I love you. I want to say more but—oh hell. Be happy, laugh in the sun, dream of me. Till soon.

That was June 1. A few days later, Maura's letter in hand, I wrote her back, or started to; I'm not sure I sent it. I said how "alienated" I was from my work; that I'd decided I would not stay at Bendix past August 31; that I had settled on Montreal to live; that I was studying French and liking it and that my pleasure in the language "reinforces Montreal and a different culture on my mind." Could we ever be free? The answer, I asserted, with not a scintilla of evidence, was yes.

Then, I added: "Here's the germ of an idea"—and simply copied out, without explanation or context, the opening lines of Judy Collins's song, "My Father," which Maura and I had heard her sing in Baltimore:

My father always promised us
That we would live in France
We'd go boating on the Seine
And I would learn to dance.

About a week later, I was in Esther's red Beetle, barreling up the Interstate to visit my parents in

New York (or really, New Jersey, to which they'd just moved). The radio blared. I was still in Maryland, just half an hour out of Baltimore, when the same Judy Collins song came on:

I sail my memories of home
Like boats across the Seine
And watch the Paris sun
Set in my father's eyes again.

Abruptly, as if for the first time, though perhaps it wasn't, it was no longer French and Montreal that stood paired, side by side, in my mind. It was French and *France*.

France, Paris, Maura.

I pulled off the exit ramp and into the next big rest area, known as Chesapeake House. I can't testify to bringing the car to a screeching stop, but in retrospect, given how it changed my life, I must have. I parked, practically ran into the visitor plaza, past the fast-food counters, straight to a phone booth, asked Information for Western Union, got them on the line, and dictated a telegram to Maura:

WILL YOU MEET ME IN PARIS IN AUGUST?

11

Rob!!
Oui, oui,
Si, Si,
Ja, Ja.
Come.
I love you. I want to be with you again soon—Soon!!

I had to quit my job, clean out my apartment, sell my car, get a passport, store my belongings, fix on just when to go, buy a one-way plane ticket; I didn't know when I'd be back.

It was the summer of the first moon landing. A few months before, NASA had sent a manned capsule on a test run around the moon. Now, men were supposed to actually land on the moon, step onto its surface, and, somehow, get back to Earth alive. It was almost impossible to imagine. When it happened, the newspapers gave it thick black two-inch headlines. Maura wrote me early that morning, Göttingen time, having stayed up all night to watch: "July 20, 1969, First Man on the Moon Day," she dated the letter. "My God, 5 am and they're walking on the moon! I don't know which is more fantastic—the fact they're walking on the moon, or that I'm watching them." I had no TV, so I went over to Rita and Howard's in the grad student dorm, and watched as the ghost-like, black and white images shivered on the screen. It was astonishing. Yet today it can seem like just a stage set for the more consequential drama that was Maura.

After her initial exhilaration, Maura grew restive, uncertain. She sang the Judy Collins song to herself. But she worried. If I couldn't make it to Paris after all, she asked of me, please, I wasn't to tell her right away. "I am so afraid everything will be taken from me." Just then, she was "confused, but feeling good and not wanting to sort things out—just letting everything float. But," she added, almost guiltily, "I can't help wondering how this book will end." I could tell her now, I suppose, except the book's not quite done.

We wrote incessantly, her letters reflecting her moods, fears, and shifting expectations. "I believe I am a little frightened by it all—it all being you." She'd had a dream, after getting my telegram, that we were in Paris, meeting for the first time since April, and that I didn't say a single word to her.

A few days later, she was caught up in a full-blown depression. For three days, she'd all but hidden in her room, physically sick, fevered. Finally, "I crawled out of bed and went to the movies." But she'd picked the wrong film to see—*Marat/Sade,* whose full title was *The Persecution and Assassination of Jean-Paul Marat as Performed by the Inmates of the Asylum of Charenton Under the Direction of the Marquis de*

Sade, which about says it all. "It wasn't very good for my present mood. It made me long for the looney bin where one can find truly sane people. Anyway, I've been hating the world." She wrote her shrink but tore up the letter. Now she was writing me. And I, with that tact and sensitivity for which I was so well known, wrote back that her letter made me happy; because for all its tortured mood, it brought her nearer to me. She wrote back gently chiding me: "I'm happy to hear that my great funk makes you feel good. At least somebody's getting something out of it."

On July 12th, she wrote of sitting by herself, with a glass of wine, feeling "mellow and sad and good," and wanting to tell me about it. August was approaching and, with it, Paris. "Rob, I need you. Please be gentle, please be kind, please care."

As August neared, Maura's letters began to include ordinary housekeeping details—a red dress she asked me to retrieve from her trunk, lab papers she needed me to get from Rita, instructions for loosening the strings on her cello: "If the pegs are frozen, knock down the bridge." But something else seeped from her letters, too, which I felt all through those few years with her. A philosophy? She would have laughed. A moral stance? "I want you to be free," she wrote me in one letter. "I want you to realize how much there is in the world...Don't even think of that factory [Bendix]. It is too below you and me and all that's really important in this life."

I want you to realize. Had anyone else said it, I'd have dismissed it as, well, maybe just a bit high-handed? But with Maura, I embraced this and similar mandates about what I needed to realize, how I was to see the world, what was important and what was not. One time she described her Göttingen colleagues as "bright as hell...articulate, deep-thinking, immature. With all that deep thinking and self-inspection, they can't see anybody else. They deal in ideas only. They are like adolescents as far as treating other people. I'm angry with them." She wanted more from them and didn't get it. She was so disappointed, so hurt, when the world let her down.

Looking at my photo, Maura judged me, reasonably enough, over-serious. But for all her love of dance and flowers, her unabashed delight in the more innocuous absurdities of the world, she was pretty serious herself, Maura was. She compelled attention. You *had* to listen to her; I did, anyway. Through her letters, or by her side, Maura became for me conscience, guide, exemplar, the voice I needed to hear that spoke for tamped-down parts of myself, her bravery an inspiration, her life a challenge and a dare. She spoke from so deep a well of sorrow and experience, so streaked with darkness and light.

For me, drawing from a shallower well, each of her glancing insights, which she might dismiss in the next instant, became for me a truth. It's not enough to survive, she used to say, it's *how* you survive. It wasn't good enough, not a high enough standard, to just get by. It mattered entirely what pleasures and joys, weirdness and warmth, you brought to life's few hours.

On July 18th, my passport was issued in Washington, D.C. I used a black-and-white photo I had taken of myself for a class assignment; I was taking an evening photography class at a local art school. I wore a light, non-descript dress shirt, open at the neck, and Greta's suede jacket. No beard, no mustache, but dark eyebrows that met in the middle, and the muttonchops often seen at the time.

August 1 from Maura: "If you haven't already looked in the trunks, would you please add to the list—one jersey, brownish, sleeveless dress with sash type tie belt. Sorry about this trivia. If you've already lost your mind over this, don't, repeat don't, worry about me or mine. Just get your sweet little ass over here...

> Have you sold your car?
> Are you flying? In a plane?
> When should I expect you?

A few days later, she was feeling down again. She'd written her shrink, but then, rereading the letter, "feared she would commit me to the big house here in Germany, so I tore the letter up. The loony bin here is just that—for raving mad people—I've already checked into it." That made her smile: "You know, there are things you check out in a new town—like the bars, discotheques, movies, and crazy houses." She'd be a wreck by the 18th, when I was coming, "but that wreck is all yours to comfort and love. I am hearing delicious descriptions of French beds which are very famous, for they are very big—for romping & rollicking."

For me, in Baltimore, the clock was ticking. I had my old life to close down. There were a million things to do. I cleaned out my apartment, storing some things with Esther's ex, whom Maura had gotten to know. I bought a ticket through Icelandic Air for Luxembourg, the cheap way to Europe back then. I got revaccinated. I got an international driving permit. I sold my car, arranging to meet its buyer at a VW dealer for the inspection.

That's where I messed up. Driving a van I'd rented to help move, I clipped the bumper of a car in the parking lot, then didn't stop, didn't tell anyone, blithely drove off; at that point, I'd barely slept in 48 hours. Someone more awake than I recorded my license plate number and next day, a police officer showed up at Bendix. I was called to the office, arrested, and driven to the police station. There, for the only time in my life, a jailhouse door clanged behind me. A few hours later, Rita and Howard arrived to bail me out. The trial was two days later. I was pronounced guilty, paid a hefty fine, and was released. None of this bothered me one bit—I was in such a fog, so sleep deprived, so fixed on getting to Paris, and Maura.

A few days later, I was on the plane. I remember little of the trip over except that the outskirts of Reykjavik, where we stopped for a layover, reminded me of the moon. The airline had thoughtfully left just enough time to indulge in a few Icelandic delights, which for me included a walk around the pretty downtown and a sauna. Then it was the second leg of the flight, to Luxembourg; and then the train across the French frontier to Paris, a trip of a few hours, finally pulling into Gare de l'Est on the city's Right Bank. And there, under a glorious expanse of glass roof above the tracks, waiting for me at the end of the long platform, at first small in the distance, then filling my gaze, and then my arms, was Maura.

12

Maura took me by the hand, whisked us down into the Metro, got us on a train headed beneath the Seine, managed our transfer to another line, and half an hour later led us up into the crowded streets of the Left Bank, the old student quarter. On wide rue des Ecoles stood our little hotel, the Familia, its name ranging across its breadth in art deco script. I was disoriented, exhausted from the trip—Baltimore, New York, Reykjavik, Luxembourg, Gare de l'Est—grateful to leave everything in her hands.

The following morning, with the two of us still in bed, there was a knock on the door of our *chambre*. It was Marie, the maid. She was a large, looming presence, an Amazon, I reckoned—big-boned and coarsely black-haired. She bustled about with whatever she had to do and then, about to leave, said something I couldn't decipher that sounded like a question.

A question deserved an answer, and I had none. I looked at her dumbly.

Maura spoke no French; I, who had studied the language in high school with Miss Mereson, passed the New York State Regents Exam in that subject, and taken lessons with Laure in Baltimore, was our resident expert. But Maria's question, if that's what it was, was opaque to me.

She repeated herself. The first time she'd said it offhandedly, but now her face crinkled up, as if to say, What's the matter? Why are you looking at me like that?

Maura was still in bed, watching me mismanage the situation.

Ça va? was what Marie had asked, and it was probably the most common utterance in the French language. Anyone learning French anywhere, ever, learned *Comment allez-vous?*," literally, "How do you go?" *Ça va?* was the truncated version of the same thing, which you could translate as "Everything all right?" or "You doing OK?" or "No problems?" That's all Marie had asked—an everyday, all-purpose pleasantry, part of the social fabric of France, the reply to which was normally just its repetition, now in the affirmative, without a rise in inflection at the end:

Ça va?
Ça va.

Fifty million French men, women, girls, and boys said it every day. There I was, trying to drill down into whatever rarefied and sophisticated question I imagined she was asking when all Marie needed was confirmation that yes, the room was fine, thank you.

It was a bad start.

Soon, though, Maura and I were doing what

other tourists, other lovers, did in Paris. We stopped at sidewalk cafés along the "Boul-Mich" (Boulevard St. Michel), a few blocks down rue des Ecoles from our hotel, the broad center of Left Bank life, dividing the 5th and 6th *arrondissements*. With the beguiling delight you'd see in her when she was clueing you in to something silly, ironic, or outrageous, Maura gave me a first lesson in Europe 101: First, you promenade along the busy boulevard, where natives and tourists at the sidewalk cafés check you out. Then you stop at a café, occupy a table, order a drink, and take in the promenade yourself. When you've had enough, you get up and rejoin the ambling throng, doing your bit for the show. This was public entertainment, French-style. And on a beautiful summer day, with the woman you loved beside you, with no responsibilities and no cares, it was a fine pleasure indeed.

For the first time in my life, I stepped inside a church, Notre Dame de Paris; Maura pointed out the great rose window of its Gothic facade. I knew nothing of churches, much less Gothic churches going back to the thirteenth century, much less rose windows.

We visited the Louvre. I was likewise ignorant of art; Maura introduced me to the French Impressionists (this was before its collection had moved to Musée d'Orsay). She was thrilled that paintings she'd seen only in books were right *there*, on the walls in front of us, just as the artist had painted them, alive with color no book could reproduce; she shook her head in delirious wonder. We went to the top of the Eiffel Tower and looked down over the city, then came down and took pictures of each other in front of it. We went to the Rodin Museum, and stood in front of *The Kiss*, and kissed.

We took the Metro, cars still divided by class, red or green, everywhere. The names of stations near the hotel warm my memory, talismans of that summer of 1969—Cardinal Lemoine, Jussieu, Maubert Mutualité. On September 2, Ho Chi Minh died. Father of the modern Vietnamese state and America's enemy in the war, Ho had lived for years in Paris. We attended a memorial service in a great hall, came away with tracts, on milk-white paper, attesting to the bravery of North Vietnamese soldiers, the cruelty of American arms, and the certainty of American defeat; we took it no more seriously than the American propaganda we imbibed at home, but this was *theirs*, and thus more flavorful.

We navigated menus thick with *assiette de cochon-naille du Tyrol* and *moules marinière*. We breathed the air of the Latin Quarter, the Sorbonne, and the other medieval colleges; we knew that here, on this historical stage the year before, had been occurred the tumultuous *événements de mai*, the Left Bank eruption against President De Gaulle's government, students facing down the police, tearing up the *pavés* from the street. We enjoyed the City of Light, in all its color and vivacity, all that legend imputed to it, living a dream as true, delicious, and free as it could have been, as it was supposed to be, as it was.

And then it was over. Two weeks after our reunion, Maura returned to Germany; she had experiments to do, seminars to attend, a troublesome thesis to write. And with her departure, that first discomfited moment in the face of Marie's simple question—*Ça va?*—became for me the enduring, painful touchstone of Paris.

In Baltimore, I'd never much wondered whether my high school French would get me by in Paris. In her two letters to me from the Netherlands, Esther wrote of feeling cut off from the States, overwhelmed by "all the crazy conversations I've had in four fractured languages." Likewise Maura: "I feel like a deaf mute and a stupid one at that. The language barrier seems insurmountable." But these reports made little impression on me.

In Paris, the problem of French did not all at once force itself on me. That I could speak little and understand less was plain from the beginning. But it grew worse, not better. I faced not individual moments, or classroom periods, or islands of French, but a vast, unending ocean of it. There was no escape. Only with the most painful effort, with regular resort to *lentement s'il vous plaît* ("please speak more slowly"), could

I grasp anything at all. The effort, when I was brave and determined enough to make it, was exhausting. Outside the sanctuary of my hotel room, there was French, and French only.

That I understood so little was only half the problem. The other half was that I couldn't say anything. The need to express, whether ideas, politics, feelings, or any passing insight, or even, for that matter, what I wanted in a *patisserie*, was all stopped up. I'd never dreamed of becoming a writer back then but, in this one narrow sense, I was one already, in my urgency to utter, formulate, and express. In French, I couldn't.

Even when I knew the words, rehearsing them in my mind, I could hardly get my lips around their alien shapes. Either that or I got them unintelligibly wrong altogether. Years later, in Paris again, to research a book in which a key event took place at the city's Bois de Vincennes, a major park, I visited a local history library. I needed information, I explained to the desk clerk, about what I pronounced as the Bois de *Vincent*—which, of course, didn't exist and got me a blank stare of incomprehension.

Now, alone in Paris, any thought or question, any grand pronouncement I just *had* to make, went unsaid. I felt incompetent. Once, even before Maura left, we were on the street somewhere, trying to figure out where to go, or how to get there. My mind froze. I didn't know what to ask, of whom, or how. A wave of surpassing shame swept over me. *Ca va?* No, I might have replied then, or almost any time over the next few months, *Non, ça ne va pas du tout,* No, I'm not doing well at all.

From the time I'd learned to talk—in the verbal funhouse that was our home in Brooklyn, all word-play, all the time—to arriving in Paris, I'd inhabited a bubble, where to express oneself was as urgent as breathing. Now it was as if I'd been suddenly struck dumb by a malicious disease. And as with those fifth-grade dancers I brought up earlier, it seemed to come from out of nowhere. Had I given the language barrier the least bit of respect, I might have anticipated it. But all I'd been able to think of was Paris and Maura and not anything that might come later.

With me in Paris and Maura back in Göttingen, and neither of us much able to express ourselves where we lived, we went back to writing letters, our New York accents sounding through the international mails. But inevitably, the relief was temporary. After each easy slip back into English—a few thoughts asserted, feelings shared, the itch relieved—I was left to the Parisians and their unspeakable language. I didn't handle it well. I wasn't brave. I didn't readjust, make new plans, push out into Paris.

Instead, I did just the wrong thing: I hunkered down into English. I sat back with my *International Herald Tribune,* the paper of American tourists and expats, in my room or over a beer in a café. Once, on rue des Ecoles, when a Bob Dylan song blared from a record store, I ducked into the doorway, relieved—ecstatic, really—to hear every nasal syllable.

Maura wasn't doing much better. She couldn't seem to get Friedrich, her advisor—for whom she'd gone to Germany in the first place—interested in her thesis. When, infrequently, they met to discuss it, usually after much delay, he'd get caught up in typos and grammar. The next experiment was what he wanted to talk about, not what she'd already done. Her progress slowed. She couldn't concentrate. Lab seminars were a bore. She hated the German cold, and didn't like the Germans themselves much better.

My letters, filled with hand-wringing and over-wrought ramblings, troubled her, too. Yet she replied with reassurance and good, sensible advice. *I shouldn't think of myself as alone. She was there, not so far away. She cared.* "You don't have to prove yourself to me," she wrote. "But proving yourself to yourself—that is a different matter.

Do you know what it is? Really know the *real* compulsion? If you don't face it, then you will have to prove yourself many times. In this area I know of what I speak: The burning desire for knowledge was not the sole motivating force behind my search of the degree.

In response to one of my missives, Maura wrote

back that, like Norman Mailer, whom she was reading at the time, I had a "flair for the histrionic." No, she assured me, I didn't have to "conquer" Paris; that was the word I'd used. I needed to let go of unrealistic goals. "Remember, no one is keeping score." Jason, her grad student friend from Baltimore, and Esther, had both felt much as I did: "The provincial American in Europe—confused, naive, lost & so terribly lonely. I still feel it." I needed to feel free to make mistakes, with French as with everything else. And, I needed to get out of my hotel room. "Nothing but depression happens when you're in your room. When I first got here, I hid in my room. I slept 12-15 hours a day!!" If it gets bad, "come here, or call me to summon me there. It isn't a defeat—just a regrouping."

She made light of my faux bravado: "Three weeks in Paris and you want to be an integral part of the community? Man, it took me years to find the community I wanted to be an integral part of in Baltimore! Relax—review your objectives in the new light of the Paris sun."

"Conquer" Paris? Was that what I was about?

Mine was the most adolescent of fantasies—that of the young man from the hinterlands, in my case Brooklyn, descending on the big city, Paris, London, or New York, and coming away its master. It's a familiar story, memorably fired into the popular imagination by the movie *Saturday Night Fever*, where John Travolta dances the night away in a Brooklyn club but yearns to conquer Manhattan, across the river. It's what legions of young men and women for generations have aimed to do in the Parises and New Yorks of the world.

～～～

These days, "New York" sometimes takes in the trendy parts of Brooklyn. But in 1959, the year I started at Stuyvesant High School, on East 15th Street in Manhattan, the age-old split between backwater Brooklyn and big city Manhattan was firmly intact. I'd grown up in Brooklyn. So had my parents. So had all my aunts, uncles, and cousins. My father's business was in Brooklyn, too. But then, Stuyvesant propelled me into the life of New York City, if only a tame, teenaged sliver of it.

Overnight, in my age 13 imaginings, I'd become a real New Yorker. Each morning I walked a block to the bus stop on Utica Avenue, the same one I'd used to get to junior high school. But now, rather than transfer to the Avenue D bus, I stayed aboard and took it to Eastern Parkway. There I got off, crossed over to its wide median, descended to the subway platform, boarded the Lexington Avenue Express to lower Manhattan, and became part of the great stream of humanity that was New York. I got on at the end of the line, so I usually wound up with a seat; to improve my chances, I became adept at positioning myself outside the train's doors just as they slid open. Occasionally, I'd sit beside another Stuyvesant kid I knew. More often, I read on the train or did homework. Sometimes, against the train's rhythmic roar, I slept, the train's pattern of shorter and longer runs between stops, especially the four minutes under the East River to Manhattan, alerting me to when I had to wake up and jump off; I never overslept my stop. Getting off at Union Square, I ducked and weaved through the underground complex of that big transfer station, trains from several lines rattling through, abuzz with commuters, aclog with hotdog and pizza counters, turnstiles clicking, gates creaking. Climbing to street level, I'd step out along 14th Street to school. Sometimes on a cold day, I'd take the interior hallway of an adjacent building, showing up in Mr. Leibel's home-room an hour and twenty minutes after heading out the door.

I was just a kid, 13, 14, and 15 while at Stuy, too young to indulge in New York's more grown-up pleasures. Still, after a day in class and before making my way back to Brooklyn, I was in the city, amidst all its grit and wonder. I shopped for cheap watches among the bargain bins at Klein's on Union Square. I traveled across the city for rifle team matches, once or twice to a meal in Chinatown, took long subway treks to see friends in distant reaches of Queens and the Bronx.

Politically, I sampled left and right; I went to a meeting of the League of Industrial Democracy, a forerunner of Students for a Democratic Society. At least one of my classmates fancied himself a Communist, signing my senior yearbook, "Yours, till the Revolution." During my brief but intense flirtation with rightwing thought, I attended a lecture by Ayn Rand, the scarily libertarian author of *Atlas Shrugged*, relished spotting "Who is John Galt?" graffiti, from the first line of the book, on a subway wall.

Senior year, I got an after-school job at a drug store at St. Mark's Place and Second Avenue, presided over by Lou and Harold Estroff, brothers as different as they come. Lou, tall and forbidding, always in what looked like the same severe dark blue suit. Harold, blond and easy-going, fond of inserting "the hell" into every utterance, as "Ah, throw it the hell out." I was the stock boy, at 20 bucks a week.

For three or four hours each afternoon, I'd retrieve toilet paper, Kotex, and Clairol hair care products from the basement, haul them upstairs through the sidewalk cellar doors, onto the street and back into the store, and stock the shelves. My other job was to deliver prescriptions all over west and east Greenwich Village (actually, this was before there *was* an East Village, when it was still just the old

Ukrainian tenement neighborhood, part of the Lower East Side). The job took me along St. Marks Place, where almost daily I'd see an old man, perched on the top step of his high stoop, a growth the size of a baseball erupting from his nose. It took me past Cooper Union, the old arts and engineering college my father had attended, where Abraham Lincoln gave the speech that propelled him to the presidency. It took me behind the city's facades.

In buildings where I delivered, I'd ring the bell to an apartment, never knowing whether, once admitted, the door would open onto an awful slum of a place or a luxurious pad occupied by some Village literary light; you could find both in the same building. My territory extended all across the Village.

Sometimes, trudging down a street by now too familiar to me, I'd grow bored; that's when I took up smoking, which I wouldn't give up for almost twenty years. After trying several brands, I settled on Benson & Hedges, because the pack asserted its pedigree as "Park Avenue, New York" which impressed the 15-year-old I was. Hell, this wasn't Flatlands anymore, wasn't Brooklyn. I was a New Yorker through and through.

It was New York Lite, this thin sampler of the city, but after three years of it, the city had its way with me, making me forever an aficionado of subways, an appreciator of the wayward and the unexpected, of anonymous crowds and abrupt discontinuities, a lover of city life. Most of each day, I was in class, trying to wrap my brain around solid geometry or physics. But I was out in the great embracing city just enough that it became part of me and I became part of it.

This was hardly "conquering" New York, but in Paris a few years later, the Stuyvesant years were something like what I had in mind.

I was still at the Hotel Familia, where even a cheap room, at maybe 200 francs a week, was eating up my budget; I had savings from my overpaid years as an engineer, but they wouldn't last forever. I moved out and, for a few nights, stayed in a cheaper room across Boulevard St. Michel in the 6th *arrondissement*, the urgent moans of a couple's lovemaking nightly drifting up through the airway.

Another place I looked at was a real garret—low, sharply sloping walls, great views of neighboring rooftops, bathroom down the hall. Finally, I responded to an ad for a room in an apartment back in the 5th, for 350 francs a month, about $65, less than my rent in Baltimore, with kitchen privileges; my new roommate, Pierre, the son of the apartment's owner, was a law student. "The Mets win the Pennant," Maura wrote back when I told her of my happy find. "I have an Introduction [to my thesis], and you have an apartment in Paris—the age of miracles has not yet passed!"

This should have been good. Sounded good to Maura, sounded good to me. My new place at 3, rue le Goff was just down the street from no. 10, where Sigmund Freud had lived in the 1880s. Practically across the street was Luxembourg Gardens, acres of greenery in the heart of Paris going back to the 17th century, virtually a stock character in French literature, dotted with little chairs for which you ponied up a few francs to sit and watch the passing scene. From the window of my apartment, I could look down at rue St. Jacques, rue Malebranche, and beyond it wide rue Soufflot and the dome of the Pantheon, the mausoleum of Rousseau, Victor Hugo, Emile Zola, and other Great Men of French nationhood.

When my friend Jack heard I was in Paris, he wrote to say that "at the very least I expect to hear you're painting on the Left Bank. Straight out of 'An American in Paris' with Gene Kelly...Doubtless you have a French mistress. Give her my love." Well, no. But I did have my iconic *Indispensable,* the faux-leather bound street guide to the city's 20 *arrondissements.* I'd stop for *croque monsieurs* on Boul-Mich, take meals at a Vietnamese restaurant around the corner. I had some money. The draft board didn't know I was here, because I hadn't told them. My room was in a large, comfortable apartment, a Robert Indiana LOVE poster on one wall, a fine view of the Latin Quarter from the adjacent window.

The problem was, once you got beyond outward signs and appearances, it didn't add up to much of a life.

At a big department store, where I could shop without having to say much, I bought a portable radio. It was a mid-priced model, a Philips, with a little heft to it on account of its heavy battery. It had eight transistors, two *gammes*, or frequency bands, one of them identical to the familiar AM band in America, the other with unfamiliar numbers, spanning a different frequency range. I'd listen to it in bed at night. Sometimes, feeling ambitious, I'd tune in to French-language broadcasts; more often, though, when I could find it, English.

That was one small comfort I enjoyed that fall. Another was a poster calendar where each month illustrated one moment in the metamorphosis of a flower—as a seed buried in snow in January, bursting forth in March, basking in the sun in April and May, blossoming in July and August, shriveling up and falling back to earth in September, its own seeds lying quiet in the earth during dark December storms, ready to flower the following year. I loved its simple, childlike renderings, its bright splashes of yellow and green, its reassuring theme of growth and renewal.

I have as much to say as I do about the calendar and the radio because I became so familiar with them both. I rarely left the room. I was doing just what Maura said not to do. Stepping out into the late autumn cold to buy roasted chestnuts from the street vendor on rue Gay-Lussac might be my only adventure of the day. I rarely saw my roommate Pierre who, though not unfriendly, was older than I, straitlaced, and busy with law school. His English almost as bad as my French, he was content to treat me as the reliable monthly rent I was.

There was a big, bright foreign-language bookstore a couple of blocks away from which I'd return laden with Dickens, John Updike, Norman Mailer's *Advertisements for Myself*, or Abraham Maslow, with his "hierarchy of needs," the idea he'd made popular. I read a lot during those months, almost entirely in English, lying in bed, little exploring the Paris streets. I am ashamed of that now. May I use that word? Is it inappropriate for anything so seemingly harmless as reading in my room, door shut, closed off from the world?

I'd hear later how the French, especially Parisians, were said to give no quarter to foreigners trying to speak their language, never helping, never stooping to English even if they spoke it, insisting on French, and good French, showing imperious disdain at the first wrongly conjugated irregular verb. It was reassuring to hear that later, and from so many people. But even so, that was *their* failing; it made mine no less.

Moved by kindred forces—her frustrations with Göttingen and the lab, my retreat from the fullness of Paris—Maura and I wrote to each other incessantly. In one letter, on November 18, she wondered,

Do you ever think that our exchange of letters may be the core of our affair? I have and I do. I just fully realized what the old romantics were doing when they were wooing by letter. It is wonderful when I read your letters. I don't interrupt. I go back over some things and reread the tender passages. I can let myself feel and express my joys and tears immediately. I don't have to worry about my defenses.

Twice I joined Maura in Göttingen, which is about as far from Paris as Baltimore is from Boston. On the train, which traced the well-trod invasion route, German border officials in peaked caps, straight out of the movies, demanded my papers. In Göttingen, I found some 1930s-era propaganda flyers, part of a numbered series, like baseball cards only black-and-white and on thinner paper, showing Hitler laughing, or embracing a wreathed German girl plainly smitten with her Führer.

I saw middle-aged and older men on the street and wondered what they'd done during the war, then only a single generation past. Many of the town's streets, homes, and public buildings still bore Gothic roots from the Middle Ages—half-timbered houses, crenellated walls, steeples and public sculpture. Maura's lab, on the other hand, was new and modern, packed with bright young faces from Italy, India, America, everywhere.

You could buy wursts in 31-flavor variety on the street, beer in the lab cafeteria. Mostly, I tagged along with Maura. Many of her lab mates did speak English and I was freed from French. Once, at a club with Maura, a favorite Simon and Garfunkel song came on, "The Boxer." Feeling its familiar arcing rhythms and warm, welcoming English, I got up and wiggled my ass to it with Maura—a virtually unrepeatable victory.

Back in Paris, I began to realize I couldn't live on Maura's letters alone, that I'd really need to learn French. So, did I push myself into the life of the city? No, what I did was cut out and translate articles from French newsweeklies—about the troubles of the automobile industry in, say, *l'Express*, or a review of an American novel in *Le Figaro*: "The French reader is at first deceived by the heaviness and sluggishness of a narrative in which the principal character is boredom. Certainly one is bored by Madame Bovary, but that boredom is absorbing. Here, it derives from a bleak sadness." This was a French critic's take on *Couples*, John Updike's novel of suburban infidelities, as I translated it with help from my Collins French-English dictionary. I'd cut out the article, tape it down on the left-hand page of my Librairie Joseph Gibert notebook, and write out my translation on the right-hand page, making a separate list of especially tricky words. When I realized it was not the big words that caused me grief but French's medley of little words and connectors—like *afin de*, "in order to," or *au dela*, "beyond"—I began to make a master list of them, which I actually took as far as the i's and j's. I pursued these strategies with modest persistence for a month or two, at the end of which I had improved my ability to speak French not one whit.

Occasionally, of course, I did manage to extricate myself from my room. I found an over-chlorinated public pool where sometimes I went swimming. I spent a day at the *marché des puces*, the great Paris flea market. Another time I met a guy about my age, from Scotland, with a thick brogue, and spent an afternoon with him at the top of the Eiffel Tower smoking dope and speaking English. I met a cheery, chubby French hippie girl, Françoise, whose English was much better than my French, with whom I sometimes palled around.

And I met Cassie, an American woman in her thirties, an ex-pat long established in Paris, who worked in public relations. She was fluent in French, but of course we talked in English. Cassie knew everybody, was hooked into everything. Noting the

imminent introduction of the Boeing 747 to international travel, she hatched a scheme for getting her
and me and whoever else bought into the idea on one
of the first flights in January. Together we drafted a
letter to Pan Am. It didn't work, but it was fun trying.
Always bright-eyed and welcoming, she invited me
once to a big party at her place where, half a dozen
conversations going on at once, I understood none of
them and, predictably, left feeling worse than had I
stayed home.

I was in over my head. Paris was too much for
me, beyond my coping skills. I was a mess, and didn't
even understand how ineptly I was flailing. I kept
doing what was easy—keeping to my room, reading,
writing to Maura, translating articles from French.
I mean, *really!* I didn't understand how the feelings
assailing me arose from choices I'd made.

Meanwhile, I was starting to run through my
money. And eventually I'd have to do something
about it. One day, about three months into Paris, I sat
down and free-associated on job ideas—place a situ-
ation-wanted ad in the *International Herald Tribune*;
thumbtack an ad in a local laundromat; even reach
for a life preserver Dad had thrown me: Nickel, a key
metal used for electroplating, was becoming scarce in
the States. Maybe, he wrote, I could track some down
in Europe.

There was another option, and this one I did
act on: Before I left Baltimore, I'd gathered some of

my best photographs, made good prints of them, mounted them on thick backing board, and created a modest artist's portfolio: A weed pushing up through the cracks of a brick patio. A trashcan lid hanging from a brick wall. Some of my better formal portraits. And a few pictures I imagined as arty, like the nude I'd done of Bev and a close-up of a phonograph needle sitting delicately in the groove of an LP. I'd heard about international photo agencies, like Magnum, of Henri Cartier-Bresson fame, which had offices in London, and arranged a brief trip there, thinking to scare up business as a photographer.

At Magnum, I was ushered into a dark office and invited to sit across the desk from a gentleman who, after a few pleasantries, set about riffling, one by one, through my portfolio of a dozen or fifteen photos. Giving a few seconds to each, it couldn't have been more than a minute or two before, reaching the final few, he was ready with his verdict...He delivered it in almost musical synchrony with his flips of each photo from one pile to the next: "Good....."—*flip*—"...amateur..."—*flip*—"...work." And that was it. He'd left me with that "good" to take home with me, yet with perfect delicacy made it clear that I and my work need take no more of his time, or that of Magnum's, whereupon I was shown the door.

I did not feel defeated by his assessment; it was as if I'd known it all along. In Baltimore, two years before, I had taken to standing for quiet minutes outside the show window of a famous portrait studio, Bachrach, near my apartment. Bachrach photos were conventional and formal, the men in dark suits who looked like they ran the world, the women decorous and discreet, in pearls, always at least "handsome" whether they were beautiful or not. I loved those portraits and finally I'd gone in, introduced myself to Mr. de la Puente, the manager, and expressed interest in working there part-time or on weekends.

Perhaps, came his reply, but first, you see, I would have to take their little test.

Now, who's taken more tests than a recent college grad? History tests on the origins of the Industrial Revolution. Calculus tests on evaluating definite integrals. Yet the test I took that Saturday morning at Bachrach's was unrecognizable, wholly alien. It came down to, *What's beautiful?* I was shown a pair of geometric shapes, A or B, and asked which I liked better. Or some object would be removed from a composition and I was asked which I preferred, before or after. Or one element was lifted a little, or lowered, relative to another. What did it even *mean* to be right or wrong on such questions? I could hardly answer A or B, because I was left so unmoored by the peculiarity of the questions themselves: On what principles were they based? Were there rules or equations for beauty? Could you look them up in a book?

I don't know just *how* poorly I did. What I do know is that for all Mr. de la Puente's easy, impeccable manners, he didn't invite me to apprentice or have anything to do with Bachrach studios.

Now, in London, having shown my work to the man from Magnum, I'd gotten essentially the same answer. I accepted it without a murmur of protest and, via a stormy trip on the ferry back across the English Channel, returned to Paris.

———

Christmas was coming. Or maybe I was looking ahead to Maura's birthday in January. Or it was one of my trips to Göttingen and I just wanted to give her something I knew she'd like. In any case, one chance comment planted the seed—that she loved sea shells. That was all it took.

I went shopping in Paris, and bought her a gorgeous oversized book, *The Shell: Five Hundred Million Years of Inspired Design*, full of lush color photos of one beautiful specimen after another. I tracked down a dealer in sea shells and bought two particularly exquisite ones. One was called *Murex Nigritus*, a big showy thing with black spiny spurs; the other was lovely but less dramatic. Maura, I was sure, would love them.

But now things got out of hand. Through photography—this was a year and a half after the Bachrach test—I'd grown fascinated by how the same face, object or scene could look humdrum if flatly lit, yet beautiful with the right lighting; portraits of Hollywood stars were sometimes the work of four or five lights— main, fill-in, and several accent lights, each carefully balanced against the others. In my basement studio across Calvert Street, I'd enjoyed fooling with the lights to create the best effect. And now, I decided, I'd do the same for Maura's seashells, with a custom-made, one-of-a-kind display case for them: The two shells would be set into the base of a miniature black cardboard theater, complete with tiny light bulbs, connected to a hidden battery, to illuminate them in what I fancied was the most dramatic way. So they'd be seen as if you were at a play, my black box being the stage set, Maura the only viewer.

This, I suppose, qualified as a loving act, a "thoughtful" gift. Maura did like it and, I learned later, kept it for years. But was there not something desperate, disproportionate, and junior-high-school-ish about it? For once I had my shells, and my art and hardware supplies, it was hours and hours back in the room with pencil sketches and dimensions, thick black cardboard, razor blades, rulers, and glue. The shell-box reprised my same tired old pattern— stay home, do something well for school, do a really bang-up Project, impress the teacher. It was another retreat back inside, while Paris pulsed outside.

Three and a half months had passed since I'd arrived in Paris, Maura was visiting, and we were embarked on urgent business. It was December 1, 1969, and that evening she and I roamed the streets of the Latin Quarter looking for the next day's *International Herald Tribune*. Sometime long after midnight, it must have been, we found a stack of them plopped down beside a news dealer. We opened it up, extracted a copy of the next day's paper, and urgently paged through it in search of a single informational nugget—one fact, one crucial number.

Earlier that evening in Washington, D.C., 366 blue plastic capsules, each containing a small piece of paper on which was inscribed one of the 366 days of the year, had been picked, one by one, from a large bowl, and matched with a number: September 14, the first date drawn, was 001. This meant that next year, when they called up young men for the military, those born on September 14th would go first. April 24, my father's birthday, was next. It was the first draft lottery, a throw of the dice that determined the fate of hundreds of thousands of America's young men. It did mine.

With a number between 1 and 100, I'd heard, you were almost sure to be called up. Between 100 and 200, it could go either way. Beyond 250 or so, you were safe. Maura and I went through the paper, looking for the list, found it, scoured it for my birthday, May 28: I was 308, which meant I had life in front of me, even though the capsules for others might mean death in Vietnam. Now, I could inform my draft board that I'd quit my job at Bendix, which would get me reclassified 1-A. So I'd be *eligible* to be called up, but they'd never get to me; that's what the draft lottery, the product of much political horse-trading, meant. Let no one say dumb luck doesn't count, or that a good life owes only to talent, ability, and hard work. December 1, 1969 proved otherwise: I'd been lucky in so much else, and now I was lucky again.

I don't remember how we celebrated, probably because Maura and I soon ran into trouble, with each other. Belatedly, I had become bothered by a troubling pattern in what we were like together. Maura, as I've said, was wont to expound, with eloquence and abandon, on anything tickling her mind and sensitivities. And I'd always lapped it up. She would go on, her voice and face changing instant by instant, about the indignities of the lab, a successful experiment, new insight into Friedrich's flawed character, or just the day's headlines.

But during such rants, I sometimes felt as if I'd disappeared. Half an hour, say, into one of Maura's more operatic performances and the thought would bubble up, unbidden, that yes, here was Maura, but *where was I?* Did she, caught up in her monologue, even know I was there? (I didn't appreciate at the time, though it should have been obvious, how similar all this was to when I was a boy, listening in rapt fascination to my parents.) My realization now began to flare into righteous indignation, and real argument. Maura, at first baffled by my anger, would come away wounded and hurt.

Meanwhile, she had her own gripes with me. Göttingen, and the lab, and molecular biology had become a prison for her. She dreamed of distant places. Why not, she'd suggested, a trip across the Mediterranean, to Tunis, for Christmas? I supply this fact solely on the strength of a letter she wrote me later, once back in Göttingen; I don't remember it myself. The arrangements for such a trip, it seems, had been left in my hands. But I had done nothing and, now in Paris, Maura was fuming. Our visit went bad, the air charged with malignity.

Finally, at some bleak juncture, wounded by one of her barbs, determined to impress her that nothing meant as much to me as she did—the logic escapes me now—I took my costly camera and heaved it out the window, where it sailed six stories down to the street and crashed into a million pieces. The two letters I got from her after this attack of insanity were dark with recrimination—but also worry that her moods were poisoning our relationship.

So things were not entirely sunny for us as we approached the end of our time in Europe. Maura had not finished her thesis. She was, though, finished with Friedrich and Göttingen and planned to return to Baltimore, to wrap up the writing, in January; the plan was, I'd come a week or so later. I didn't know just what I'd do back in America, but the lottery had left me safe from the draft, and in any case I'd be with Maura.

But first, before Christmas, we met in London. We visited the House of Commons and saw the fiery young Irish nationalist Bernadette Devlin deliver one of her rousing speeches. With Maura, I celebrated my first Christmas, the two of us exchanging small gifts in our London B & B room. It was a great old place, one I couldn't help but imagine living in a hundred years before. Maura brought me up short, saying, "Well, I'd have been the maid."

From there, we took the train to Glasgow, where we stayed with Maura's relatives. A poor place it was, in a run-down neighborhood, with an icy cold bathroom, but warmed by New Year's cheer, and drink, and much madcap instruction in the hows and whys of haggis and the intricacies of a Scots brogue: *Aye, and it's a braw, bricht, moonlit nicht.* Someone had a car and drove us around town, proudly pointing out every last statue, factory, or public building, every faintest wisp of local lore. Maura and I, in the back seat, squirming, politely oohed and ahhed. This was the world of Maura's mother, and it was as foreign to me as anything I had seen in France or Germany.

Soon, after clearing out my Paris apartment, in a blur of travel I little recall, I was back in Baltimore; Maura, who'd flown back with her thesis from

Germany a bit earlier, got us a temporary room at Reed Hall, a faceless high-rise dormitory on the Johns Hopkins medical campus in East Baltimore. We stayed there a few days or a week, then found an apartment together. That was where the bad times spun out.

13

You'll understand if, right off, I don't want to talk about them—maybe like a soldier reluctant to recount his combat experience and live through it all again. Something unutterably beautiful went missing. Who'd want to read so grim a story? Who'd want to write it? And yet from the crumbling chrysalis of my relationship with Maura emerged, over the next twenty months, my new life.

Despite that last sour stretch in Paris, when we first got back to the States we were still mostly OK. "I didn't think I would miss you so much so fast," she wrote, her letter reaching me just before I came over myself. "Over the Atlantic I realized that we should have flown together...I want you here. I need you here." Before I arrived, Maura stayed with Rita and Howard in McCoy Hall, where I'd watched the moon landing in August. Now we found our own place, in a brick, four-story building that we moved into at the end of January: One bedroom, on the top floor, with a tiny kitchen, a dining alcove just off it, and a good-sized living room. It looked out onto the back parking lot of the city schools administration building next door, so we'd routinely be woken by cars starting up, revving, screeching. We sweltered through the summer. We learned to make home-made yogurt on the stove. With her sewing machine, Maura made me a stunning silk batik tie, in intense shades of blue, with blood-red flowery accents and peach-colored lining. I made a clunky green canvas bag and a pair of navy pants that never fit and I never wore. Here we lived almost until the end.

And here I lived a new beginning, too, and became a writer—not because I decided to become a writer, but because I began to write.

The U.S. hadn't yet invaded Cambodia nor had National Guard troops shot and killed four war protestors at Kent State; that would come in May and, with it, new waves of anger and rebellion. By now, 48,000 Americans had been killed in Vietnam. The March on the Pentagon had been eclipsed by much larger national protests. Johnson was long gone. Nixon appealed to his Silent Majority, but the counterculture was everywhere. Even in behind-the-curve Baltimore, "head shops" sold incense, herbal lotions, marijuana paraphernalia, and whatever else you'd never see at a big department store. American society had split in two.

It had split not, as in the recent Trump-poisoned presidential elections, between urban and rural, or between the coasts and the interior, but between the generations—a "vertical" more than a "horizontal" fissure. For me and most of my friends, marijuana was just fine, Scotch the business of sad old men. Bob Dylan was our voice, Elvis Presley a relic. Laid back spontaneity was great, nine-to-five was death. Margaret Mead wrote a book about how, for the first time, grandparents had everything to learn from their grandchildren, not the other way around. The generation gap, the newsmagazines called it. Marked by mistrust and confusion between baby boomers and their parents, it was vast, pervasive, and real. We couldn't talk to each other—or worse, didn't know what each other was talking about.

Just then, I didn't feel that way toward my own parents; I'd get to *that* later. Born in 1946, I was among the oldest of my generation. The Depression and the war years were almost as alive for me as for my parents. Their experiences and values sat in fragile communion with my Sixties-rooted ones of peace, justice, liberation, and love. I didn't see either as "wrong" but, rather, both—impossibly, simultaneously—as right.

I was thinking about these things one day in February, a few weeks back from Paris, as I walked along 25th Street, near our apartment. This worn, unlovely stretch of street had homes, a few shops, and some social service agencies, like the American Friends Service Committee, the Quaker group that had advised me about Canada. But whatever they were, they were all accommodated in 15-foot wide porch-fronted row houses like those you saw all over the city.

In front of one of them, I saw a sign for *Harry*, which happened to be my brother's name but was also that of Baltimore's underground newspaper. Something like its bigger city cousins, the *East Village Other* in New York, or the *Great Speckled Bird* in Atlanta, *Harry* was the counterculture's answer to the city's big dailies. It had no reporting staff. It had no discernible journalistic standards. It made no pretense of objectivity. Its comics were angry and out-rageous. It raged against the war, the Establishment, racism, and injustice. *Harry* lasted only a few years but, just then, it was wholly of its time.

And I, at that one odd moment, was wholly of my time, too: I stepped in from the sidewalk, up onto the porch, rang the bell, and was greeted by a young man not much older than I. This, it seemed, was the editor, Michael Carliner, who invited me in. I rattled on about all the things I was thinking about. He let me. He listened. Well, maybe I could write about all this stuff? *Did he ask me, or did I ask him?* I don't know. But the answer, in any case, was sure, why not?

This, astonishingly, was my start as a writer—a start portended by not a single thought, ever, that I might become one.

I delivered three essays under the collective title, "A Primer on the Roots of the Cultural Alternatives"; its grandiosity mirrored both youth culture generally and my own overwrought sensibilities. The first piece, which appeared in late February, got its own cartoon: "OK," says a crotchety middle-aged guy, cigarette dangling from his lips, waving a finger at a bearded youth, maybe his son, "so you want to end the war, end racism, end poverty, and end pollution. But what about something POSITIVE?"

My piece started with two lists of about fifteen words each—"stock market," "profit," "technology" and "control" on one; "peace," "harmony," "flowers," and "love" in the second. No word on either list, I asserted, could be comfortably imagined on the other; they *belonged* together, grouped in these clumps. And so distinct was the gulf between them, mirroring the two "cultural alternatives" I aimed to describe, "straight" and "hip," that no one could wonder about which words went where.

Behind that gulf, I said, lay the differing economic roots of the generations. The "capacity to produce goods," I declared from the lofty perch of my 24th year, was a solved problem. Straight people (as the term was used then, without reference to sexuality) had been traumatized by the Great Depression, when the economic system had broken down and there wasn't enough to go around, and remained mired in their collective memories. For them, the natural "yearning for a warm bed and full belly has been perverted" into obsessive regard for economic plenty, at the expense of all other values—values like the peace, harmony, and love the counterculture sought to confer on the gray, sadly stunted, straight world.

My essay was convoluted, needlessly abstract, and violated every precept of good writing practice. (And Norman Mailer had used the list device, I realized later, in a book I'd read in Paris.) But it got printed, and it had my name on it. The next two essays, appearing at two-week intervals, developed my theme: While the industrial system keeps us "regimented, orderly, proper, rational, predictable, and clean—in short, machine-like—hip society responds with its experiments in drugs, music, intentional community, study of Eastern religions, mysticism, and rejection of the nine-to-five job."

Here, then, was my "primer," the explanation I'd been good enough to bestow on my handful of readers. That it wasn't good didn't much matter, because it was the beginning. And also because, between the first and third pieces, I called Mom and told her what I was up to—that I was writing something important to me, and that I enjoyed doing it. My poor mother, of course, had seen in my letters the depths of abstraction into which I could sink. "You know," she said gently, "you might want to get hold of a little book to help you. It's called *The Elements of Style*, but everybody just calls it Strunk and White," after its authors.

A book of just 71 pages, Strunk and White went back to the 1930s. It consisted of Will Strunk's writing advice to his students at Cornell, together with a new fifth chapter, "An Approach to Style," by the great *New Yorker* writer E. B. White. I had never heard of it. I had never taken a writing course. I had never received ten minutes of writing instruction. Strunk and White was by this time a classic, many a happy soul in the humanities and the arts having imbibed its wisdom. But not I, Rensselaer Polytechnic Institute, class of 1966. Maybe earlier I wouldn't have been so ready for it; but, now, in February 1970, I was writing something I cared about. I was primed. It all made sense: *Omit needless words. Use the active voice. Write with nouns and verbs. Do not overwrite. Do not overstate. Be clear.* I read it through and even by the third of my *Harry* essays, it was helping me pull tangles of weeds from my overgrown prose.

Its principles seized me at once—in a way that much of what I'd presumably learned about taking photographs, for example, had not. The Bachrach aesthetics test I'd found so unintelligible had a happy aftermath, leading me to often ask myself over the years why one scene, image, or arrangement seemed attractive while another did not. But those lessons came hard. In Strunk and White, I similarly came face to face with an aesthetic practice's mature wisdom. But this time it *took*, immediately. Here was revealed truth that no one had bothered to reveal to me before.

Of course, I'm still sometimes brought low by

sins Strunk and White condemned; you'll no doubt find examples here. And back then, certainly, and for some time to come, I was as inexpert a writer as I was a photographer. But my delight in that little book, the pleasure I felt in applying its maxims, told me a new story, with unaccustomed force and clarity: Despite all the flabby, inchoate letters I'd written Maura and my clumsy essays for *Harry*, words and ideas were my most natural home. I enjoyed thinking hard about what they meant, listening to them, playing with them, hanging out among them.

Besides, I was a published writer now, if only in *Harry*.

⌣

Meanwhile, Maura was back in the lab, doing experiments and working on her thesis, or trying to.

A doctorate in the sciences from a research powerhouse like Johns Hopkins was a years-long undertaking, with no unobstructed path to its completion. Courses taken as part of your graduate studies might be much like those you'd taken for your bachelors and, often enough, no big deal. But you didn't get a doctorate for taking courses; that was the least of it. You got it for discovering something new. Maybe not something big, but *something*. Even with a supportive advisor adept at guiding you along productive lines of research—and Maura felt she never had that—it was a long, uncertain haul. There was nothing automatic about it. Experiments failed all the time. Or they "succeeded," but only in undermining your hypothesis. Or, especially early on, they served your advisor's larger research agenda more than your own.

And then there was the thesis, or dissertation— two or three hundred pages, with charts, tables, graphs, and bibliography, describing your research, placing it in context, addressing likely objections, nodding respectfully to your scientific predecessors. Obtaining a Ph.D. taxed the resources of even gifted students. In the biological sciences, it might take four or five years to complete—or six or seven. Maura had been at it now for more than six. In Göttingen, she had been writing her thesis, but only fitfully, and still had scientific holes to plug.

She worked in an unremarkable mid-rise building in the Johns Hopkins Medical School complex in east Baltimore, a fifteen-minute drive from the apartment. The lab was crowded with refrigerators, burners, scales, sinks, and hoods, ordinary gray metal desks piled high with equipment catalogues, flasks, beakers, test tubes, and ice buckets. And beyond the background clutter of any lab, there was specialized equipment, like ultracentrifuges, which spun test tubes at high speed, separating out components based on molecular weight. Or electrophoresis units, where sample solutions set out on a piece of special filter paper were fractionated by electric charge, their molecular components "migrating" to distinct spots on the paper.

Molecules, of course, were invisible. But this was still biology, which meant that rats or worms or fruit flies supplied biological material. For Maura it was rabbits, which were delivered to the lab from time to time and from which she'd extract blood. And not just from adult rabbits; she needed tissue from rabbit embryos and fetuses as well.

In these years, the primary object of molecular biology was determining the structure of key proteins. Hormones are proteins. So is the collagen of skin. And so is hemoglobin, the oxygen-bearing molecule in the blood of mammals. Hemoglobin turned out to be a group of linked helical chains that together formed a kind of pocket for holding oxygen; figuring it out got two British researchers the 1962 Nobel Prize in chemistry. But there were important variants in hemoglobin structure. The hemoglobin in an embryo, for example, typically differed from that of the adult animal. Maura had found a variant of rabbit hemoglobin marked by two additional amino acids. She'd gotten this far but now, it seemed, was stymied.

⌣

Just back from Europe, I began looking for another engineering job. Inoculated from worry about the draft, I had the whole of American industry before me. I got interviews with a few local firms. One was American Totilisator, the company that made display boards for race tracks. Another was an outfit that made corrugated boxes—not exactly high tech, but the machinery to make them could be interesting. I didn't get either job.

But then, further into the year, I was no longer looking for an engineering job at all. Nor was I doing anything with photography. In fact, the raw evidence might suggest I was trying to be a writer, though I said nothing of the sort to anyone, and probably didn't even think it.

In March, Maura and I drove to Maryland's Eastern Shore to view a total eclipse of the sun. I wrote an essay about my moment of atavistic dread as the sun disappeared, but no one published it. Later, I flirted with writing a piece about philosopher Herbert Marcuse's idea of "repressive sublimation": Capitalism took political passions and ground them into safe commodities, as in rage against the System reduced to T-shirt slogans. That went nowhere. With Maura, I wrote a piece about Summerhill, the self-directed learning approach championed by the English thinker A. S. Neill; we got it published in a tiny local publication, *The Paper*.

And I launched a little project where I viewed TV commercials, tracking how they reinforced Establishment values like reverence for technology and women's-place-is-in-the-home; I sent a piece describing my home-grown research, "The Sponsor is the System," to the *Saturday Review* and other publications; I got no takers. All these early writerly efforts bubbled up ingloriously from my one paper-thin success, those raw rants for *Harry*. At some point, I wrote a piece, extracted from my engineering days, about how defective merchandise got into the world. "Too often nowadays, that shiny new toaster, air conditioner, or television set doesn't work the way it's supposed to—or breaks soon after you buy it..." And this piece did sell, to the Sunday supplement of the Baltimore *Sun*, earning $75, my first pay as a writer.

At our local library, a fine, old Victorian heap of bricks a block from the apartment, I found a book called, approximately, *How to Become a Freelance Writer*. It said you could do some initial research on a subject, write a "query" letter to an editor, and get an assignment. It talked about the "lead," the beginning of a piece aimed at hooking the reader's attention. You couldn't just sound off, you had to think of your reader, what she wanted and needed. It wasn't much about writing mechanics; I had Strunk and White for that. Rather, it was nuts-and-bolts practical, holding out the prospect of actually getting paid for your writing, even making a living at it.

This was a new idea.

In April, I took what I'd learned from the

freelancing book and wrote a query to *Baltimore* magazine. I'd recently seen two newspaper reviews of the same play that differed completely, as if they were about two distinct animals entirely. How could this be? Does a critic's opinion mean anything at all? What do critics really do? To whom do they owe their allegiance? Armed with these and other questions, I suggested an article about the city's theater and film critics. The editor wrote back, asking that I call him to talk it over.

At a bar across the street from our apartment, I planted myself at a pay phone, organized my papers around me, and dialed my first real editor. His name was Bill Stump. He'd come up through newspapers, I'd learn later, but now was trying to remake *Baltimore* magazine, published by the Chamber of Commerce, into a serious publication; in his own way, he was trying to mend the generational rifts I'd written about in *Harry* by introducing new ideas and odd corners of city life to conservative business readers.

Later, he'd get fired for doing that too vigorously. But now, on the phone, Bill seemed to welcome my ambitions for the piece. It would probably appear in the fall, he said, just as the local theater season opened. They'd need finished copy by mid-July. *Baltimore* was no *Life* or *Look*, he allowed, but they could pay $125, which was more than a month's rent for Maura and me. He'd send me the magazine's style sheet, along with other articles on theater criticism he'd collected.

I had a deadline, a word-length, and an agreed-upon fee. I was on assignment!

The Hamilton Street Club was a revered old gentleman's club in the venerable Mt. Vernon neighborhood, inhabiting a row of connected brick buildings along little Hamilton Street. There I met R.P. Harriss (once an assistant to H.L. Mencken, the Sage of Baltimore), who was soon batting out stories from his long life in theater and literature and opining on all matters critical. From there, it was Rob Kanigel, boy journalist, tape-recorder spinning, on to the more proletarian-minded Lou Cedrone, cigar-smoking R. H. Gardner, and other local lights from the worlds of theater, film, and journalism. Here, the way I introduced them, was the local Cultural Establishment. To the public, they remained "flesh-less and abstract. What," I promised to answer, "are they like behind their bylines?"

I didn't know what I was doing, but I did it—transcribing notes, working through structural problems, struggling with what to leave in and take out, ideas in my head butting hard up against facts. "The job teaches you," my grandfather used to say. It took way too long, but gradually the article took shape and, benefiting from Bill's gentle editorial ministrations, it appeared that fall, along with photos of my subjects, across eight of the magazine's creamy, coated-stock pages.

14

When we'd first met, Maura told me about her deep depressions, which had left her hospitalized a year or two before I'd met her and afflicted her still. Mostly, though, I hadn't seen them up close, not enough, anyway, for me to inhabit the bleakness with her. But now, living with her on St. Paul Street, I did. Her face, usually so kinetic with life, sometimes just shut down, went blank and dead. Her speech, usually so expressive and unguarded, would flatten, disappear. She wouldn't speak at all.

Once, in our first days together in Baltimore, I'd asked her, in all innocence, whether she could control her moods. She reminded me of my question in a letter from Göttingen, answering it this way: "It's only fair to inform you that these depressions—these destructive depressions—still come over me, and I have lots of difficulty controlling them." She was on tranquilizers. Her episodes didn't persist as long as they once did, "but I am still prone to my bad self. If you can't take the bad, please don't play around with the good.

"And don't gloss over the bad," she added. "It can get pretty wicked. And it is always directed at the person I love most—so, baby, you're it!" But not to worry, she brightened. "By the time you read this and reply, I'll be bouncing around again...But what I really wanted to say was that I can't promise you a rose garden"; she was nodding to Hannah Green's semi-autobiographical 1964 novel about mental illness, which she'd had me read—"and that you'll have to accept." *Accept?* Of course, I did. By now, I'd all but promised her my eternal love. Besides, the worst of it was over, right? With us, in our love together, we could surmount any obstacle. I picture Maura chuckling ruefully.

Now, lost in a darkness of experiments that didn't work, paragraphs of scientific writing that wouldn't cohere, and a new Hopkins advisor who had no time for her, Maura's depressions deepened. Certainly they didn't yield to anything I said or did. In my experience as adult friend and lover, I was a one-trick pony: If something was the matter, you talked about it. Out of that talk, presumably, came understanding, empathic connection, insight, and relief. That was it. I didn't know how to do it any other way. I wasn't able to just let Maura stew, in her own fashion and in her own time, lending her support until she emerged. I didn't respect her own knowledge of herself. I didn't wait for her to talk, but *pushed*, insisting on some expedited path to catharsis and resolution.

But now there *was* no resolution. I'd never seen such deep, disabling sadness. I asked questions but got no answers. So I'd ask again. At first gently. But in time, in the face of her silence, I grew accusative: *Why won't you talk to me, Maura? Just talk. That's all.* To this, when she was feeling as down and discouraged as she often was during these episodes, I got nothing. When that failed, I bludgeoned. *Maura, for God's sake, how can we work this out if you won't tell me what's going on with you?*

Silence.

Maura?

Silence.

Maura, please.

Silence.

I began to take her want of response as an insult to *me.* I'd get angry, accuse her of not even trying to pull out of it. *All I ask is that you talk to me, and you can't even do that?*

Of course, battering at the thin armor of her silence, I only caused more damage. So now, whenever she did manage to speak, it was often hurtful, leading to a further downspinning spiral. "Did we invent sex?" Maura had written to me once from Göttingen after the first great days in Paris. But now, during these episodes, she couldn't stand to be touched, much less warm to sex; this, of course, divided us the more. I felt the awful distance, which I didn't know how to separate from coldness. No matter that it was all she could do just to keep going.

I didn't understand any of this and so embarked on a kind of research program. I went over to the

Welch, the big medical library near Maura's lab at Hopkins, and studied up on depression, which Maura had explained to me was different from simply feeling unhappy or blue. Hers, plainly, went way back. She'd told me about what being abandoned by her father had meant to her. Her mother, of course, paid the price, too, her own bitterness ladled onto her only child, threatening to leave her when she wouldn't behave; Maura felt doubly abandoned.

Now, in the Welch stacks, this new subject, depression, *was* interesting, and I *did* learn. About, for example, the "flat affect" I saw in Maura on these occasions. About the difference between exogenous depression and endogenous—the first arising reactively, on the back of outside events, the other from within. Oh, I learned a great deal. But it left me no better able to help Maura out of her misery, or me out of mine.

For I wasn't doing well, either. My emotional repertoire was so narrow, my resilience so readily overcome. I was supposed to be the "normal" one of us—good Jewish boy, middle-class home, intact family, deep wells of healthy optimism. Maura had pointed to blots in the pretty picture, her fine-tuned sense of injustice and slight challenging me to see my mom and dad through new, more critical eyes. I had been uprooted from my third-grade class and dumped into the fourth grade, my friends left behind, and my parents had never even *asked* me? In fifth grade, a year younger than everyone else, I was actually *surprised* everyone knew how to dance but me? And Stuyvesant? Unfamiliar new faces again, no girls, and that long schlep into Manhattan every day, while my junior high friends remained companionably together back in the neighborhood? What had *I* had a chance to say about going to Stuyvesant? Was I given a choice at all?

Maura had grown up in her little Staten Island house, Mrs. McNair, its formidable regent. But I had my own, less evident scars, my childhood leaving me sometimes feeling compliant and small. My family roots felt no longer quite so healthy. And when I, or Maura and I, drove up to visit my parents, these new confusions and uncertainties sometimes fulminated into anger.

Myriad pathologies floated through our apartment on St. Paul Street. From the beginning, Maura had represented a challenge to me, but now sometimes the challenge cut deeper, felt malign.

⌒

In June 1970, a chubby, 4' 10" Polish-American social worker from the streets of East Baltimore named Barbara Mikulski made headlines at the United States Catholic Conference when she declared that America was, for southern and eastern European Catholics, no melting pot but rather "a sizzling cauldron." The ethnic American was "sick of being stereotyped as a racist and dullard by phony white liberals, pseudo black militants and patronizing bureaucrats." Ultimately, Mikulski would be elevated to the U.S. Senate, where she'd serve for more than 30 years, making her the longest-serving female senator when she retired in 2016. But back then, she was still largely unknown—a lively, blunt-spoken, unelected activist who'd helped block an expressway from ramming through her neighborhood and now was taking her first steps onto the national stage.

Bill Stump knew a journalistically good thing when he saw one and asked me to interview her. The format was the one pioneered by *Playboy*—an introductory verbal portrait followed by questions-and-answers distilled from the raw material of a much longer interview. "I think we're on the brink of moving back to ethnicism," Barbara told me. "Because we find American culture so sterile, so unliturgical, so uncelebrative, that we're going back to our own stuff." The interview was later reprinted in *Catholic Digest*. Later, I helped her write a piece about her childhood, "Growing Up Ethnic," for *Redbook*.

By late 1970 and early 1971, I had a steady diet of work. I wrote about *The Whole Earth Catalog*, "Guide to Tools for Life Outside the System," as the headline in the Baltimore *Sun Magazine* called it. I watched movie scenes of explicit sex for an article about Maryland's Movie Censor Board and interviewed

Mary Avara, its head, a Baltimore bail bondswoman magnificent in her warmly twisted logic. What did she mean by "filth" and "dirt"? I asked her. "It's not art. Art is beautiful. My father came from Italy where the famous artists come from." I profiled an activist Goucher professor, wrote about a controversial radio call-in show, covered a ban on rock music at the local civic arena, and interviewed an FCC commissioner for whom television was simply "mind pollution."

The internet did not exist. My research forced me out of the apartment, into the surreal basement offices of the censor board, to City Hall, to Baltimore's Penn Station, where arrivals and departures were still recorded in chalk on a blackboard. Were I writing now about Don's candy store back in Brooklyn, I'd *have* to go inside it. My work gave me license to go where otherwise I might not have gone, talk to those I otherwise might never have met, even confront some of my personal demons: Years later, I would write a long article about the traps and difficulties of learning a foreign language.

Bill Stump at Baltimore magazine launched a column, "Transition," to bring alternative points of view to his creaky readership; to him, my youth made for my best credential, suiting me to write on children's reading habits, war-to-peace economic conversion, or alternative education. I devoted one column to a review of Alvin Toffler's best-seller, *Future Shock*, about how the very pace of change—not only what it was changing to or from, but the sheer speed of it—left people unmoored. So *that* made me, of course, a book reviewer, and soon I was writing 800-word reviews for the *Baltimore Sun* on books like Benjamin DeMott's *Surviving the Seventies*, yet another attempt (and a good one) to make sense of the country's troubles.

It was a heady time, me at my pea green Smith-Corona, which my parents had given me when I was 11, set up on an old drafting board stretched between the trunks I'd brought back from Europe— it, and I, forever clattering away. I wasn't making much money. I was still learning my craft. Articles took time to research, then sometimes couldn't find a welcoming editor. Publications that did accept my work were mostly local and, by New York standards, ill-paying.

A year earlier, as an engineer, I'd made $850 a month. Now I was happy to get a check for $125. Book reviews paid $15, plus the book. But it wasn't just Bill Stump who saw promise in me; half a dozen editors had published my work by now. Each day I consorted with our language. I was meeting interesting people, reviewing significant books, venturing to odd, unexpected places. For all my natural reticence, I was out in the big world now. I didn't want to be anywhere else.

One day about a year after I'd started along this road—articles appearing with my byline, small checks arriving almost regularly—I solemnly declared to Maura that I was going to be a writer. Asked about it much later, Maura remembered the declaration, remembered the solemnity I brought to it. What she didn't remember—couldn't have, because the whole idea is ludicrous; it didn't happen—remains etched in my memory anyway: I was *kneeling* as I said it, as if proposing marriage.

That's odd enough. Odder still is that I'd never imagined myself a journalist, poet, novelist, intellectual, author, or any other kind of writer—never even as arrant fantasy. I'd taken my first steps as a writer by simply taking them. It was only in retrospect that it began to make sense: In college, I did well in courses requiring papers; sometimes I helped other students with theirs. My only "A" in a technical course came in a strength-of-materials lab where your grade depended solely on the term-end report. And then there was my spontaneous attempt at "journalism" at the mine disaster site in West Virginia. It revealed no hidden talent, or even ordinary, workmanlike skill. But my need to get something off my chest and onto paper—*that* was there.

For someone who, as it turned out, would make a life, and career, as a writer, it's astonishing how awful my earliest writing had been. I have only to look at letters I wrote Maura but never sent. Or, college papers that, at their worst, were incorrigibly abstract, miasmas of word-games and backings-and-forthings so thick I was lucky anything intelligible emerged at all. Yet I enjoyed doing them. Nothing else felt so natural to do.

I'd felt close to few of my teachers at Rensselaer, but one exception was Professor Traschen, a fellow New Yorker with whom I'd taken two English courses in senior year—Dostoevsky's *Notes from Underground*, Ionesco, Pirandello, Beckett's *Godot*. After graduation, I wrote to him about the war, my weapons work, and other themes alluded to in this book. Just a few days before I left for Paris, he wrote me: "What I'd like to see you do when you get a chance is an article for a magazine on your change, one focusing on the subtle details of your developing consciousness, your new sense of things." I didn't do it, but I suppose he'd seen enough in the gawky, earnest outpourings of my letters to encourage me.

It was not just the writing itself that kept me on track but the taste it gave me of the freelance life, with its peculiar mix of freedom and uncertainty. Freelancing means getting up late? Goofing off? Writing when the spirit moves you? That's one vision of it—and a sure prescription for failure. Early on, I became hyper-vigilant about my time and how I used it. I realized soon that interviews, hours in the library, and other research took as much time as the writing itself, and that time-sucks and distractions loomed everywhere.

Almost from the beginning, I made money—or a

little, anyway, enough to contribute to the household pot. But it was a different kind of money, each check intimately tied to a particular project—the subject I'd written about, the people I'd talked to, the places I'd gone, the editor I'd worked with, the pleasures or frustrations of the writing itself. Though at the end of the month it added up to much less than I'd ever made as an engineer, every dollar seemed to matter more.

Once out of high school, I'd turned my back on Ayn Rand, but one of her ideas stuck with me. In her novel *The Fountainhead*, architect Howard Roark agrees to design a housing project for Peter Keating, a mediocre but well-connected society architect who lands the big jobs while he, Roark, gets by on the rare client who appreciates his genius. Roark makes but one stipulation: Keating can take the credit and pocket the money, but the housing project must go up exactly as he's designed it. Of course, it doesn't; it's a mess. So Roark dynamites the still uninhabited project. In court, his defense is simple if a little wacky: He'd never gotten the satisfaction of seeing his architectural vision go up in steel and stone; his "fee" had never been paid.

In other words, the pleasure of doing work that interests you, turning down work that doesn't, and doing your work in your own way, was part of your pay as artist, freelancer, entrepreneur. I was never so pure as Howard Roark; who could be as pure as one of Ayn Rand's unhinged heroes? I learned to listen to what editors said and to improve my work. But during my first years as a freelance writer, this idea was deeply meaningful to me.

What I wrote for *Harry* in 1970 was almost the last I would do for free. My new path was eased by savings left over from my engineering days; I wasn't strangled by want. Later, it would be harder. But never then, and never since, have I held a job as staff writer or reporter. I was a freelancer, and proud of it. And I was an entrepreneur, too, wasn't I, with my own scraggly little, bare-bones, ill-paying Kanigel Industries, its product words?

On the first floor of our apartment building was a bar named for the Clark Street Garage, renowned in the annals of crime as the site of the St. Valentine's Day Massacre in Chicago. One evening I went downstairs to a party there. It may have been an early campaign event for Barbara Mikulski, on her way up. Maura didn't go. At some point, amidst drinks and conviviality, I got to talking with a young woman who, in the usual way, asked me what I did. What was I supposed to say? I wasn't an engineer anymore. What I did was write magazine articles. So I said that. Her eyes grew large with interest.

In those days and for years thereafter, I never called myself a writer; that was for poets and novelists. I abjured the noun altogether and invoked the verb: I said I *wrote*, then said what I wrote. But it didn't seem to matter much. That I wrote anything,

anything at all, seemed to land me on a higher rung of the sexual-romantic pecking order. Engineers were way at the bottom, down among the accountants.

It was 1970 and I was the same person I was the year before. But that I was a writer now was enough to lift my market prospects. It wasn't fair.

Of course I didn't mind.

———

Meanwhile, Maura and I limped along. We saw her friends from folk dancing and from the lab. We drove to D. C., where we bought hand-made leather sandals. We went to a workshop on male chauvinism; this, at the dawn of the modern women's movement, was still a new idea. As with all things Maura, I embraced her Scottish roots; we attended the nearest Scottish Games, with their peculiar athletic events, like throwing the caber, and where I, Robbie McKanigel, thrilled to the pipers playing "Scotland the Brave."

On one trip we stayed with Maura's mother, in Staten Island; Mrs. Muir would alchemize any wisp of doubt, discomfort, worry, or controversy into a cup of tea. In August, Maura and I made the long drive up to Acadia National Park in Maine, where we watched the waves crash onto the rocky shore and camped on Cadillac Mountain, witnessing, as promised, the first rays of morning sun on North America. We ate lobster on the dock—until the barest snatch of French from the next table put me on instant alert and unsettled our meal. The Maine air was fresh, godly, and pure. One afternoon, I lay out alone under the blue cloudless sky, briefly freed from the weight of our lives back in Baltimore.

For Christmas that year, Maura gave me a record, an LP, Beethoven's *Ninth Symphony*. I listened to it again and again, imagining I heard in its first three movements a searching, or struggle, that could only be resolved by its glorious, choral "Ode to Joy." I knew next to nothing about classical music, and I was still only a journeyman writer, but I had begun to think about structure, shape, and form.

So Maura and I managed. Not well, but we were getting by, until Chrambach and Rodbard stepped into Maura's life, and therefore into mine.

⁓

They sound like names from a Samuel Beckett play, but they are real, unchanged here. Andreas Chrambach and David Rodbard were researchers at the National Institutes of Health who had pioneered a new lab technique for separating the components of proteins. It was called polyacrylamide gel electrophoresis, bore a family resemblance to the older paper electrophoresis, and would become a standard lab technique around the world. But this was still early

1971; the journal article that was its founding document would not appear until April. Until then, if you wanted to use it, as Maura did, you had to learn it, step by step, with all the special reagents and protocols, at the elbow of the scientists who had developed it, just as a stage magician learns tricks not from books but personally, from other magicians.

Chrambach, who had first worked out the method at Johns Hopkins, and his collaborator, Rodbard, were based in Bethesda, 40 miles down the road from Baltimore. Maura made one or two exploratory trips there. And then, at some point that winter, early in 1971, she began staying down there, for days or weeks at a time, at the Bethesda apartment of her friend Diane, an artist and folk dancer who'd recently broken up with her boyfriend. Soon, Maura was all but living with Diane, talking into the night about Diane's life and, no doubt, her own.

Maura duly explained to me the need for all this, though by now I felt only a little more aggrieved by her physical distance than I'd become by her emotional distance. Most of her things remained at St. Paul Street, and she'd return periodically. But now, of course, it was that much harder to bridge the chasm between us. I found it hard to be infinitely understanding, and impossible not to feel sorry for myself: *She can talk with Diane till all hours, but she can't talk with me?* And our old standby, our delicious, wooing letters? We didn't write.

When she was back in Baltimore, it was more of the same. After one fight, Maura stalked off—to the car, I supposed, parked on St. Paul Street, which no windows of our apartment faced. So I ran from the apartment, into the hall, and up the stairs to the flat asphalt roof, crossed over to the building's St. Paul Street side, and spotted her, small on the sidewalk four stories below, striding determinedly. I stretched myself over the parapet and yelled, "MAUUURR-UH!," drawing out the syllables, straining, my throat made raw by the effort. "MAUUURR-UH!" She momentarily looked up but kept walking.

Just as my ineptitude in French had drained and deflated me, so did my confusion about Maura. Where had this new thing, our deteriorating relationship, *come from*? It was incomprehensible to me. I used that word a lot when I got angry with Maura— that this or that in her actions was incomprehensible to me. And it was—so far outside the narrow range of my thin adult experience. How could life take this awful turn, our love ground down into something so sad and miserable?

I was certainly as much to blame as Maura—more so, probably. To adapt the lyrics of the old Beatles song, I'd taken a sad song and made it worse.

By late spring 1971, the NIH work paying off,

Maura had moved her thesis along, the holes in its scientific fabric mended. She was close now. For some months, I'd periodically driven out Harford Road to deliver parts of her manuscript to a professional typist. On July 23, I picked up the last of it from Mrs. Platt, gave her a check, and brought Maura's thesis home to her.

Things began to move fast now, energy blocked for so long released into action.

First came Maura's thesis defense. You write a thesis and you "defend" it before several of your professors—orally, in person, taking questions. It sounds scarier than it was for her. Generating the data, doing the experiments, forming arguments—that had been hard. But now, the defense came almost as anticlimax. She got through it fine. She was going to get her degree. She'd be Dr. Maura McNair. By this time, I so identified with her struggle that I'm sure it meant as much to me as to her. Maura just wanted it to be over, and now it was. It was a huge accomplishment. By any professional or academic standard, she was a success.

But in the human and personal ways that also matter, it had defeated her, defeated us both.

All this time, she'd been arranging for a postdoc— one more hoop, one more interim status, between student and full-fledged researcher; she got one at the Scripps Institute in La Jolla, California. The plan was to drive out there that summer, together;

whatever we thought privately, we weren't talking about splitting up. Maybe neither of us had the guts to mention it. We rented a small U-Haul trailer, packed it full—it had my KLH stereo and my new French ten-speed bike—hitched it to *Schatzi*, Maura's dark gray Volvo, with its Barbara Mikulski sticker on the rear bumper, and drove over the Appalachians, across the Midwest, over the great plains.

I was secondary to the big move, and I knew it. After all, I could work anywhere—write about anything, freelance from California as well as Baltimore. At the time of our trip, I was working on an article about efforts to arm Congress with tools to help it control new technology. By the time we left, it was not quite finished, so I worked on it along the way: There I was with my Smith-Corona and drafts of the piece sprawled across a park bench in Iowa.

We stopped to see an old friend of Maura's in Colorado. In Wyoming, Big Sky country, there was nothing for miles, nothing but nothing; I didn't like it. One morning we woke up to icicles in our tent. We spent a day or two in Salt Lake City; it had liquor stores, which surprised me.

At the California line, we posed for snapshots beside a road sign heralding our arrival. For New Yorkers in the Golden State for the first time, California could seem exotic. Maura, in her short flowery dress, stood straight and tall beside the sign. I leaned against it, in sunglasses, wearing the beret

Maura had given me, with its colorful embroidered label inside, like those made in the factory where Maura's mother worked.

We stopped for a few days in Berkeley, to visit Maura's friend Diane, who had just moved there from Bethesda. The California hills were *brown,* not green; I didn't get that. Los Angeles, of course, was what everybody remembers—the sprawl, barreling through it at sixty miles an hour and never getting to the end. Finally we reached San Diego, our destination, where the air felt lighter, as if there were less of it.

The trip could have been exciting or fun, and left us closer, the two of us together as the great country sped past. But it wasn't. The past year's bad feelings and distancing had taken their toll. Spurts of nastiness bubbled up in Kansas, in Colorado. I was with Maura, but I wasn't. She was setting out on a new life that had no room for me.

A day or two after we arrived, the fragile cord of our relationship snapped. One more dig, one more little hurting remark, another conflagration. I took a long hot shower. When I got out, I told her it was over. But in all the little ways that matter, she'd been telling me that for months.

15

I called Jack, my friend from both high school and college, who lived in Los Angeles. After college, Jack had joined the navy, seen the world and met the Indian-American woman, Asha, he would later marry. I don't know how I got up to LA, my temporary asylum; for all I remember, lost in a fog of loss, I could have been teleported there. What I do remember, from that first Saturday morning at Jack's, were the lawnmowers, chattering across the neighborhood. I woke up thinking, Aren't the suburbs supposed to be quiet?

Jack was a wise-assed New Yorker not about to be brought down by his lovelorn friend; there'd be no soulful sharing with my old buddy from Kissena Boulevard. In fact, if Jack offered any remedy for a broken heart, it was to get me a date. Her name was Nancy, and all four of us were soon headed off for Disneyland. I couldn't stand the place. There we were, in one corner of it, Happyland or whatever it was that Walt Disney had snapped his fingers and willed into existence, surrounded by robotic young men and women obsessively sweeping up litter, rides promising thrills and adventure, a made-up world giving the finger to the real one outside its gates.

It wouldn't be the first time someone too fussy

or critical had descended on Disneyland and, under the relentless California sun, failed to appreciate it. For me, just then, a few days after breaking up with Maura, all I could do was revile and reproach it. I grew frantic, made myself obnoxious to Jack, Asha, and Nancy—until finally I apologized to my friends, arranged to meet up with them later, stepped into a booth or shop, begged a pen and paper, retired to as quiet a spot as I could find in the middle of fucking Disneyland, and proceeded to write a fat, formless missive about its evils, excesses, and sins, eight pages of it. It was no contribution to the scholarly literature of Disneyland, I assure you. But I had to get it out, purge myself of a little misery.

And then, having written it, I folded up my rant, packed it away, tracked down Jack and Company, and for the rest of the day had a grand old time amid the cheerful surreality of Disney's astonishing creation; I was, for the moment, cleansed. On one ride, some sort of high-concept sliding-board, Nancy behind me, her legs flanking my shoulders, I felt the slightest, most innocent erotic tingle as we slid down in happy abandon.

Bless Disney.

Bless Jack, and his rude, rough ways.

At one point, aching for Maura, I phoned her. I'm not sure I asked her whether we should try again, but I must have sounded her out. Maybe it was all a mistake, but any lingering irresolution passed, and the next step was to get back to San Diego and do all that had to be done to sever our lives from one another. Money. Belongings. Return the trailer and sign up for the van I'd need to ferry my things to San Francisco, five hundred miles up the coast, where I was bound; I wasn't about to turn around and head back east again.

I woke up early the morning I was to leave, Maura sleeping beside me, the Peter, Paul, and Mary song, "Leaving on a Jet Plane," drumming obsessively in my brain.

All my bags are packed
I'm ready to go
I'm standin' here outside your door
I hate to wake you up to say goodbye
But the dawn is breakin'
It's early morn
The taxi's waitin'
He's blowin' his horn
Already I'm so lonesome
I could die.

If you want to get all literal about it, the song had little to do with me and Maura—no jet plane, no taxi, no honking horn. But every word, every note, burned. I loved Maura as much as ever. But now we were miserable together, and we were finished, and I was leaving. I'd have months, and all the years ahead, to try to understand my loss.

16

There is another story I might tell here, of the drive up to San Francisco; of the city's remarkable beauty; of cable cars and the Golden Gate; of writing successes and failures; of encounters with die-hard Lefties, Army recruiters, and rich folk from Marin County; of pretty women and love affairs; of lying in bed alone in my apartment on Green Street and listening to the fog horns moan.

But all that begins a new story, one hinting at easy continuity, moving blithely ahead. On the surface, that's what San Francisco was for me, what I wrote back to my parents to say it was. That's how it might have seemed to me a few innocent years earlier—of moving along in healthy growth and mounting maturity.

But it wasn't that way at all. I was not moving ahead. I was stuck, aching for Maura, writing long letters to myself, trying to understand what had happened, to me and to us, how she'd become my very blood, and how I'd lost her. And all the while, as I explored the city, and worked, and met new people, I tried to be as good and brave as she would have wanted me to be.

We corresponded. Occasionally, during the three years I lived in San Francisco, we'd spend a day

together. We once met in the peaceful green precincts of the Shakespeare Garden in Golden Gate
Park. Another time I hitchhiked to San Diego to see
her. After a while, Maura drifted away from science.
She became involved with other men. She traveled,
especially in Bolivia, where she befriended the native
Andean peoples there and flirted with the illicit world
of *coca*. Later, she married. She lived well, had a
child, adopted another, divorced, lives today in the
deep south, and dances.

We still write sometimes. For my birthdays, she
sometimes sends me one of those oversized greeting
cards that, through a tiny speaker tucked into its
cardboard anatomy, booms out loud, lively snatches
of Marvin Gaye or *The Messiah*.

A few years back, Maura came to visit, staying
with me and my wife at our house in Baltimore. She
was coming down from New York, where she'd been
visiting one of her daughters. I picked her up at the
train station. She was in her seventies now, looked
great, and soon was regaling us with stories of life
down south.

Dylan Thomas once prepared a film script about
a fisherman, Maurice, on an isolated Irish island,
known as the Great Blasket, and his unlikely friendship with a college student, George, from England.
But this George, though an Englishman, was not,
Thomas decreed, to be portrayed unsympathetically.
Because for Maurice, he was "the voice of the world

beyond the Blasket horizon. He is the voice that is heard in all man's growing up: 'There is a world beyond your own.'"

For me, that voice was Maura's.

For years, even when I started this book, I'd seen my love affair with Maura and my wayward migration into a writer's life as two distinct stories playing out on separate tracks, the merest accident of timing. But those tracks coincided *exactly* in time. Maura was there at the beginning, with all my first hesitant steps. And it was to her I'd declared that day, in full operatic measure, that I would be a writer.

Now, it's plain to me that my turn to Maura and my turn to life as a writer stemmed from the same impulse—the wish, and need, long tamped down, to venture beyond all I'd known as a boy within the embrace of my parents, and to engage with people, places, and ideas in the big world beyond theirs.

During my years as a writer, I've never written much about myself, except in a few light personal essays. Nor did I set out to write this memoir. But beginning about a dozen years ago, when I was in my early sixties, from time to time I'd cast my mind back at a memory, find that I wanted to dwell on it, open a computer file and record some random fragment. The fragments accumulated. They were always about those few years abutting 1969. I came to think they might add up to something. And so it was that, at the end of almost half a century of setting words to paper and screen, I discovered one more subject I needed to explore—my own life. Not my whole life, just those few early years in Baltimore and Paris.

It was three years ago that I mostly completed the account you've read here. Writing it gave me much to think about, maybe too much. A "coming-of-age" story is, I think, the result—one that, however different from others of its kind in family, locale, chronology, and event, justifies the term. Such stories all tell of First Days, of times more dramatically lit than others coming later: For me, it was the first time really on my own. First job. First consuming love. Groping my way toward meaningful work and a place in the world.

My story has left me to look back at a version of myself I often cannot admire, someone a little stupid and insensitive, who knew so bloody little and erred so often. But, as if in recompense, it has also let me look back at my younger self—body fitter, skin unblemished, emotional "witness plate" not yet so stained and scarred by adult trials—and to live that boy's life afresh, as it never would be again, reborn.

Much has filled the half century since those years of 1969: San Francisco; back to Baltimore; Cambridge, Massachusetts; back again to Baltimore. Lovers and friends, two marriages, one son, stepchildren, accidents and bouts of ill health, books read, books written, ideas debated, travel, bicycling thousands of miles, plays seen, much Bach and more Dylan, meals savored, a few serious personal crises along the way—in short, the familiar, recognizable stuff of a life, some of it disappointing, or harrowing, some of it that I won't soon, or ever, be ready to write about (whether for the shame of it, or the stain on others) but much of it, too, deeply satisfying. Overall, a lucky life, never in real danger, never in true want.

The years since have at times been just as eventful as those I've written of here, but they rested on the bedrock of 1969. As the years passed, I came to view myself not as an old boyfriend of Maura's, but—as I've described, in all grandiloquence, "The Man Who Loved Maura." And eventually I came to realize that I was not just writing, not just doing a different sort of work from what I'd prepared for in college, but I had actually become a writer; not just through hours spent at the keyboard, but as my identity.

Now, fifty years later, I am proud of the work to which I have given many of the best hours of my life. But I suspect that Ingmar Bergman's character, Isak Borg, was proud of his work, too. He might well have said or thought something similarly prideful about his own work—work he approached, it seems, with enough devotion and success to be honored for it near the end of his life, culminating in that road trip to Lund to accept his laurels.

This likeness, it should be plain by now, is a fraught one for me, especially as I reflect on my life, now, at almost the same age, and stage of life, as that old professor. Giving myself to the pleasures and frustrations of work, among my books and papers, alone with words and ideas, happily caught up in the intriguing subjects and stories my work affords me, I made some of the same choices Isak did. I chose, deliberately, to give time and attention to my work, and not always so much to others, leaving me to reap too large a harvest of loneliness and chill.

The crowded fireplace mantle of my office holds a few artifacts and mementos from my life—old cameras; souvenirs of a film they made from one of my books; the blue and white polka-dotted belt from a thin cotton robe Maura once wore; a black-and-white photo of me at age 14, wearing a Stuyvesant sweatshirt, aiming an old rifle as my father looks downrange through binoculars at whatever I am shooting at; the little radio with the *gammes*, or European broadcast bands, that I bought in Paris and listened to alone in my room. Meanwhile, on a shelf by the window sits the pea-green Smith-Corona typewriter on which I did my first writing.

Today, I live with my wife in a Baltimore rowhouse, a specimen of this old city's vernacular architecture, up Calvert Street from where I first lived as a tenant of Mr. Heidler in 1966. It's one of 23 on our side of the street—16-feet- wide, porch-fronted, built in 1906, not far from where Maura and I lived when we got back from Europe. From the front, except for their sometimes raucous paint jobs, they are virtually identical. But inside, or as seen from the back alley, the years have altered them with parking pads and room extensions, walls and decks, gardens and planting. Sitting out on our back deck, facing the alley, I find a peculiar comfort in the view, cluttered though it is with power lines, trash containers, and trees left sick and bedraggled by the years. It's close-in and intimate. I know many of my neighbors up and down the alley, look out on them from our deck.

Sometimes I walk down to 25th Street to pick up a prescription or a sandwich. I go out the back door, through the garden, down the alley, turn at the elementary school at the end of the block, and amble past the basketball courts. There, on any summer's day, the boys are shooting hoops—sneakers squeaking, the big ball passed, dribbled, thudding on the asphalt court. Sometimes I stop for a moment to watch, but then, invariably, continue on my way.

YOUNG MAN, MUDDLED

ROBERT KANIGEL

ACKNOWLEDGMENTS

This book started out about 15 years ago as raw fragments of memory. Ed Barrett, an MIT colleague, saw some of them, and encouraged me to dip into what was for me a new genre, memoir.

More recently, I owe thanks to Rachele, Laird, and my wife, Sarah, for helping me to see what I hadn't been able to see on my own. And also to Pat McNees for driving it all home in a particularly rough, honest, and useful way.

Thanks to Bruce Bortz at Bancroft for getting behind this book all these years after he'd published my earlier book, *Vintage Reading*; to his capable intern, Elizabeth Redmond, for her editorial care; and to Pamela Mensch, for taking so much interest in this book and helping to make it better.

I've changed names and identifying details of several people who figured in my life back then and appear in these pages now.

ABOUT THE AUTHOR

ROBERT KANIGEL is the author of nine previous books, most recently *Hearing Homer's Song: The Brief Life and Big Idea of Milman Parry* and, before that, *Eyes on the Street*, his biography of Jane Jacobs. He has received many awards, including a Guggenheim fellowship, the Grady-Stack Award for science writing, and an NEH Public Scholar grant. His book *The Man Who Knew Infinity* was a finalist for the National Book Critics Circle Award and the Los Angeles Times Book Prize; it has been translated into more than a dozen languages and was the basis for the film of the same name starring Jeremy Irons and Dev Patel. Kanigel and his wife, the poet S. B. Merrow, live in Baltimore.